Note to the Reader and Acknowledgements

A knowledge of the two novels is assumed throughout. A knowledge of more of Jane Austen's works would be extremely useful.

Please note that the reader is referred to as 'he' in the interests of economy rather than of sexual discrimination.

Sydney Bolt, Joyce Ditzler and Flavia Gapper have been extremely helpful in various ways.

I Introduction

1 Jane Austen and her Society

'She had bought him a copy of *Little Dorrit*, and insisted that he read it. He had started reading the introduction, by an academic, thinking it was the novel itself, and as a result abandoned the book as useless.' Thus a modern novelist (Peter Ackroyd) on the futility of explaining the classics. And Jane Austen is no less a classic, no less funny and popular than Dickens. She is probably easier to read. Nevertheless it is useful to ask questions about her art, to consider how she achieves her effects and what, apart from good entertainment, those effects are.

Like many novelists, Jane Austen appears to offer a picture of real life: places we might have gone to, people we might have met, types we may even encounter as yet. But how true is she to the England of her time? Here is a passage from *Evelina* (1778) by Fanny Burney, an admired predecessor in the art of polite fiction. In a setting which might be mistaken for something out of Jane Austen, the heroine narrates the following scene from high society (Lord Orville is the virtuous hero):

Before dinner came Mr Coverley, and before 5 o'clock, Mr Lovel and some other company. The place marked out for the race was a gravel-walk in Mrs Beaumont's garden, and the length of the ground 20 yards. When we were summoned to the course, the two old women made their appearance. Though they seemed very healthy for their time of life, they yet looked so weak, so infirm, so feeble, that I could feel no sensation but that of pity at the sight. However, this was not the general sense of the company, for they no sooner came forward than they were greeted by a laugh from every beholder, Lord Orville excepted ... For some time the scene was truly ridiculous; the agitation of the parties concerned, and the bets that were laid on the old women, were absurd beyond measure ... When the signal was given for them to set off, the poor creatures, feeble and frightened, ran against each other and neither of them able to support the shock, they both fell to the ground.

Lord Merton and Mr Coverley flew to their assistance ... Again ... they set off and hobbled along, nearly even with each other, for some time, yet frequently, and to the inexpressible diversion of the company, they stumbled and tottered; and the confused halloaing of *'now Coverley!' 'now Merton!'* rung from side to side ...   (Letter LXIX)

And so on. The passage ends: 'We then went to the drawing-room, to tea.' This is by no means the most boisterous incident in *Evelina*. The brutal behaviour of the two young aristocrats and the company of ladies and gentlemen is not held up for approval – far from it. But the novel was praised by Dr Johnson precisely for its fidelity to contemporary life – indeed that formidable authority 'repeated whole scenes by heart', an extraordinary compliment for a novel of that time. So, given that it is an accurate presentation of almost contemporary behaviour, why is there nothing even remotely like it in Jane Austen? The most physically violent scenes in her novels are Harriet's encounter with the gipsies in *Emma* and Louisa's fall from the Cobb at Lyme in *Persuasion*. Consider the former. Harriet staggers in, 'white and frightened', on the arm of Frank Churchill:

> A young lady who faints, must be recovered; questions must be answered, and surprises be explained. Such events are very interesting, but the suspense of them cannot last long. A few minutes made Emma acquainted with the whole.
>
> Miss Smith, and Miss Bickerton, another parlour boarder at Mrs Goddard's, who had been also at the ball, had walked out together, and taken a road, the Richmond road, which, though apparently public enough for safety, had led them into alarm. – About half a mile beyond Highbury, making a sudden turn, and deeply shaded by elms on each side, it became for a considerable stretch very retired; and when the young ladies had advanced some way into it, they had suddenly perceived at a small distance before them, on a broader patch of greensward by the side, a party of gipsies. A child on the watch, came towards them to beg; and Miss Bickerton, excessively frightened, gave a great scream, and calling on Harriet to follow her, ran up a steep bank, cleared a slight hedge at the top, and made the best of her way by a short cut back to Highbury. But poor Harriet could not follow. She had suffered very much from cramp after dancing, and her first attempt to mount the bank brought on such a return of it as made her absolutely powerless – and in this state, and exceedingly terrified, she had been obliged to remain.
>
> How the trampers might have behaved, had the young ladies been more courageous, must be doubtful; but such an invitation for attack could not be resisted; and Harriet was soon assailed by half a dozen children, headed by a stout woman and a great boy, all clamorous, and impertinent in look, though not absolutely in word. – More and more frightened, she immediately promised them money, and taking out her purse, gave them a shilling, and begged them not to want more, or to use her ill. – She was then able to walk, though but slowly, and was moving away – but her terror and her purse were too tempting, and she was followed, or rather surrounded, by the whole gang, demanding more.
>
> In this state Frank Churchill had found her, she trembling and conditioning, they loud and insolent. By a most fortunate chance his leaving Highbury had been delayed so as to bring him to her assistance at this critical moment. The pleasantness of the morning had induced him to walk forward, and leave his horses to meet him by another road, a mile or two beyond Highbury – and happening to have borrowed a pair of scissars the night before of Miss Bates, and to have forgotten to restore them, he had been obliged to stop at her door, and go in for a few minutes: he was therefore later than he had intended; and being on foot, was unseen

by the whole party till almost close to them. The terror which the woman and boy had been creating in Harriet was then their own portion. He had left them completely frightened; and Harriet eagerly clinging to him, and hardly able to speak, had just strength enough to reach Hartfield, before her spirits were quite overcome. It was his idea to bring her to Hartfield: he had thought of no other place.

This was the amount of the whole story ...   (Chapter 39)

This incident is a little alarming, of course. 'It was a very extraordinary thing! Nothing of the sort had ever occurred before to any young ladies in the place, within her memory; no rencontre, no alarm of the kind ...' Emma reflects. But it is hardly the stuff of heroic fiction: and, indeed, like the incident at Lyme, it is often criticized for its bald and summary treatment of the action. Like that too the real interest lies elsewhere, in the reactions of the characters to unusual events. For Emma (and therefore in a way for poor Harriet too) it starts off a new notion of romance: 'It had happened to the very person, and at the very hour, when the other very person was chancing to pass by to rescue her!' For the alert reader it raises the question as to what Frank and his scissars were really up to at Miss Bates's house. Our conclusion must be that Jane Austen virtually excluded the rougher aspects of life in her society *quite deliberately*. Partly, no doubt, because she disliked them, but chiefly because they offered nothing of interest for her art. John Thorpe in *Northanger Abbey* might conceivably have been present at the scene from *Evelina*; and Mr Elliot's black past might have contained it – but one rather doubts even that. Jane Austen insists on offering more interesting, and positive, matters for the reader's enjoyment.

If violence plays so little a part in her novels and can be shown to be excluded as a matter of artistic policy, does this not raise the question of how much else is left out, and why? It does indeed. One of the major topics in any discussion of Jane Austen is that of her severe limitations of range and subject – limitations, perhaps, of knowledge. How much do we know about her and why does she seem to some to be too genteel?

Jane Austen's life need not detain us long, nor is as much known of it as could be desired by enthusiasts. Our main sources are her *Letters* and a *Memoir of Jane Austen* by her nephew, J. E. Austen-Leigh (1870). Of the former, many, and presumably the most intimate, were destroyed by her elder sister Cassandra after her death and probably in accord with her own feelings about privacy. Nearly a century afterwards Henry James made bonfires of letters: nowadays the tendency seems to be to put everything – everything – on tape of some kind, though perhaps reports are exaggerated. The *Memoir* is similarly permeated with family reticence,

11

but it is still very informative (and touching), and is most usefully reprinted in the Penguin edition of *Persuasion*.

She was born in 1775, one of a large and closely knit family, and the daughter of a scholarly and witty clergyman. The Austens were gentry and very well connected, though not themselves rich. Her childhood appears to have been extremely happy and full of literary pursuits – reading, acting in private theatricals, and writing. Although she remained unmarried and latterly became a kind of universal aunt, she did not lack suitors in her youth. The image of her as a withdrawn, perhaps catty, spinster is most misleading. The novels for which she is famous were essentially written, amid domestic bustle, between 1809 and 1816, although the 'early' three were extensive revisions of previous drafts. She died of Addison's disease in 1817. By then she had provoked a little fame and a good deal of appreciation: 'That young lady had a talent for describing the involvement and feelings and characters of ordinary life which is to me the most wonderful I ever met with ... What a pity such a gifted creature died so early!' wrote Sir Walter Scott in his Journal (1826). She was also patronized by the Regent in a hilarious correspondence with his librarian and was obliged in loyalty and courtesy to dedicate *Emma* to a prince she could scarcely have admired. Throughout her life Jane Austen was a devout, though never a showy, Christian. Beside this quiet life and the quiet life which is apparently (but often only apparently) reflected in her novels we should put the most obvious large-scale facts of the era in which it was lived. The result is a disconcerting sort of double vision. For, of course, it was a time of upheaval unmatched (fortunately?) in European modern history at least until the present age. One has only to murmur the phrases 'Industrial Revolution', 'French Revolution', 'Imperial Expansion', 'Napoleonic Wars' to appreciate this. And these are only the largest phenomena. I invite the reader to place side by side ideas of contemporary cotton mills, slave plantations, the fearsome London mobs, the guillotine, the battlefields of Austerlitz, Borodino or Waterloo, with ideas of the outing to Box Hill or the removal from Kellynch to Bath, and leave the rest in the hands of the historian. Meanwhile it is obvious that certain kinds of selected information from outside a work are often desirable and palpably enhance our appreciation and evaluation. It is useful in reading *Persuasion*, for example, to know what the Battle of Trafalgar was, what a landaulet was, what were the Game Laws in the early nineteenth century – and so on. It is true that without such knowledge only a little would be lost. It is also true that the work itself supplies – in a strange way that works of art have, travelling over time and space – a sense of how we ought to react to the important petty details of the scene. Nobody need tell us, from outside the work, that Bath was a fashionable resort at that time, or that Milsom Street was a fashionable shopping place, or that Molland's was a fashionable shop. It would take an extremely dim reader to fail to take this in – even if it is forgotten immediately. But even so a far more extensive, though general, knowledge of the period, of its literature, and of Jane Austen herself is a help. On intellectual matters the reader may be referred to Marilyn Butler's *Jane Austen and the War of Ideas* (1975), where the novelist is convincingly shown to be at least alert to, and perhaps a partisan in, the ideological struggles of her time.

What of the smaller aspects in which the society of the novels differs from our own? These are undoubtedly more important here than World History of the grandiose kind: and the most important of them, as any reader of the two novels will be ready to admit, is Class. This is a hot subject, and never more difficult to deal with than among those whose moral or political objections to a social hierarchy, and the distinctions adjunct to it, prompt them to deny or blur its existence. Its prominence in Jane Austen leads also to two of the worst possible readings: that which delights in the contemplation of a secure and cosy world of past elegance, the world of the refined 'Miss Austen' (known to her self-appointed familiars as 'Jane'); and that which, with corresponding crassness, rejects the whole business as too trivial, limited and smug for the attention of (equally self-appointed) serious minds. Probably most honest readers would admit to having belonged at least momentarily to both schools.

But, although the question of class will not go away, we can easily clarify it. First, it is necessary to emphasize that the attitudes and structure shown in the novels existed and that Jane Austen, as a realistic writer, is obliged to recognize and describe them. Second, we have to examine how they are used in the furtherance of her art.

First, then: the assumption of the superiority of some people over others was as prevalent in early nineteenth-century England as the assumption of the equality of mankind is with us today. That both assumptions are extremely partial and rickety and frequently bogus is obvious. Equally obvious is the fact that, perhaps especially in the earlier case, such ideas are felt as more *natural* the more they are challenged. Jane Austen's age was one in which many people did not have surnames (or 'sirnames' as she significantly spells it); it was also the age when the 'Rights of Man' had become a crusading slogan. The naturalness of class assumptions was further strengthened by the fact that they were inherited, traditional and, above all, accepted by the majority of all classes. It would be silly – although it is tempting – to view the lower orders as made up of people who felt persecuted and resentful. It is indeed a commonplace paradox that servants tend to be shocked by the frivolous progressiveness of their masters. People in Jane Austen often envy the status of others and in more or less comic ways aspire to share it, but nobody questions its existence and very rarely its justice. We have no reason to think that she was misrepresenting a society which she knew so intimately. That she was severely critical of it does not mean that she did not share its fundamental values. It is we, in the role of assertive democrats, who are historically eccentric.

Arguments for and against social hierarchy are not really to the point here. It is not the function of the literary critic, as literary critic, to reason why on such matters. In any case, the famous fourteenth-century rhyme:

> *When Adam delved, and Eve Span*
> *Who then was the Gentleman?*

is a useful hint that rational objections to automatic deference or sub-ordination are not new. But we should nevertheless note, before leaving the subject, two important limitations in Jane Austen's chosen range which, in turn, must determine the width of our response. The hierarchy evoked is social, but only social. We are scarcely concerned with direct power as opposed to status. Money, of course, gives power but it is not necessarily linked with position. Mrs Elton in *Emma*, for example, is clearly not a lady in the sense in which Jane Fairfax is. Yet she attempts a financial patronage which is rightly felt to be odious. More subtly, Mr Rushworth is clearly the richest man in *Mansfield Park* (or indeed in all Jane Austen's works – he has an income of £12,000 a year); but he can hardly compare as a fine gentleman to Henry Crawford (£4,000 a year) or Sir Thomas Bertram. And the 'grandest' of Jane Austen's figures, Mr Darcy and Lady Catherine De Bourgh in *Pride and Prejudice*, although rich, only marginally exert direct power through patronage in the Church and the Army. Second, as this last example powerfully suggests, both status and direct power are not at all the same thing as personal merit. Even leaving aside momentarily the question of personal gifts, one of the chief features of traditional society was at least a residual sense of the Christian doctrine of the equality of souls. And although this may often seem merely theoretical in other accounts of the period it is implicitly endorsed with vigour in Jane Austen. So much, so pervasively, and so obviously so, that it is reasonable – though not to me wholly convincing – for D. W. Harding to claim that the 'Cinderella theme' is basic to her novels.

The second and more important question about Class is: How, given her material, did Jane Austen exploit its possibilities? How does she use its conventions in the service of her own artistic conventions? The short answer to this is that social gradation provides one of the most fruitful opportunities for the exercise of her particular genius: it is, as it were, a ready-made system in which she can show how the fine sensitivity and intelligence of her best characters operates in contrast to the blundering insensitivity of her worst. It is a splendid framework rather than a prison.

Perhaps the best way to illustrate this is to confront directly the general impression – applauded or deplored – of her narrowness, her limitation of range. Faced with this, her admirers often produce an idiotic banality to the effect that she 'wrote about what she knew'. This is true: it is also tautological. How do we know what she knew? Because she seems to know what she wrote about. The same would apply if she were the author of successful novels on Polar Exploration. And, further, its truth is only limited. Jane Austen clearly did not 'know', in the sense of having experienced it, what it was like to be a substantial landed magnate, an empty-headed and scheming young girl, a prig, a lawyer, or even a married woman. She had met such people and deals with them and their like. But this does *not* mean that she failed to exercise her imagination. She chose – and this is a word to be stressed – to write about those parts of their lives which gave her the chance to create and analyse the areas of value which seemed to her, and seem to us, important: love, marriage, discrimination, elegance of mind, charity, wit, selflessness, taste, courage, patience, cheerfulness – and all the gradations of their opposites. Responses to Class, as I say, are an excellent field for the display of such qualities.

Limitation of range in art is, of course, not exclusive to Jane Austen. The very act of everyday perception involves, we are told, the automatic selection of significant details. We literally do not see what some part of our mind deems irrelevant. And selection for the artist becomes a necessary principle. The celebrated experiments with 'stream of consciousness' have had only a limited and dubious success. Much of what is experienced in life is superfluous and obfuscating in art – beside the point, in the fullest sense. Who has not been bored by the detailed and insignificant depictions of the minutiae of, for instance, eating, or walking, or fighting, in bad art? There are things we do not need to be told, things which get in the way – even if the subject is unfamiliar, as in the finer points of bee-keeping. And artists work in conventions which they both inherit and create. Oddly enough, the conventions of realistic fiction, the most apparently easy and available form, are sometimes the most misleading. Reading Shakespeare presents many problems as well as pleasures, but what never seems a problem is the fact that the characters, while appearing human, speak in blank verse. *A fortiori* it is not ludicrous (well, only sometimes) when people in opera sing. But in a novel, which cunningly presents itself as being far closer to the texture of 'reality', the reader may encounter a much more secretive convention. For example: if, apart from the violence I have already discussed, Jane Austen were really presenting 'what she knew', then why does she very largely exclude servants, whose omnipresence must have made up so large a part of the experience of her class? Beaumarchais – known mainly to us through the mediation of Mozart in *The Marriage of Figaro* – shows servants as virtually dominating their masters; many of Dickens's most famous creations are servants; and so on. But Jane Austen is a realistic writer who chooses to exclude not only direct consideration of the grand questions of the day but a large part of its routine existence as well. Shakespeare often chose to convey his meaning through the actions of princes; Jane Austen conveys hers through those of the gentry and their immediate adjuncts. We might speculatively apply here, *pari passu*, an impressive memory of Ford Madox Ford about Henry James:

> The Old Man knew consummately one form of life; to that he restricted himself. I have heard him talk with extreme exactness and insight of the life of the poor … But he knew that he did not know enough to treat of farm labourers in his writing. So that, mostly, when he discoursed of these matters he put his observations in the form of question: 'Didn't I agree to this?' 'Hadn't I found that?'
>
> But indeed, although I have lived amongst agricultural labourers a good deal at one time or another, I would cheerfully acknowledge that his knowledge – at any rate of their psychologies – had a great deal more insight than my own. He has such an extraordinary gift for observing minutiae – and a gift still more extraordinary for making people talk. I have heard the secretary of a golf club, a dour silent man who never addressed five words to myself though I was one of his members, talk for twenty minutes to the Master about a new bunker that he was thinking of making at the fourteenth. It was the same with market-women, tram-conductors, ship-builders, labourers, auctioneers … But he needed to stand on extraordinarily firm ground before he would think that he knew a world. And what he knew he rendered, along with its amenities, its gentlefolkishness, its pettinesses, its make-believes. He gives you an immense – and an increasingly tragic picture of a Leisured Society that is fairly unavailing, materialist, emasculated – and doomed. No one was more aware of all that than he.

People often fail to observe that many contemporary novelists are equally or even more selective.

Let us now look at a few simple examples of the result. When Sir Walter Elliot learns of Anne's intention to visit Mrs Smith instead of spending the evening with the cold-stricken Lady Dalrymple he suddenly shows an unusual concern for the doings of his daughter:

> 'Westgate-buildings!' said he; 'and who is Miss Anne Elliot to be visiting in Westgate-buildings? – A Mrs Smith. A widow Mrs Smith, – and who was her

husband? One of the five thousand Mr Smiths whose names are to be met with every where. And what is her attraction? That she is old and sickly. – Upon my word, Miss Anne Elliot, you have the most extraordinary taste! Everything that revolts other people, low company, paltry rooms, foul air, disgusting associations are inviting to you ...'

And he concludes in the presence of an embarrassed Mrs Clay:

'... an every day Mrs Smith ... To be the chosen friend of Miss Anne Elliot, and to be preferred by her, to her own family connections among the nobility of England and Ireland! Mrs Smith, such a name!'   (*Persuasion*, Chapter 19)

This is, of course, yet another instance of Sir Walter's foolish pride. And his speeches always have a diverting comic pomp. But there is, typically, more in it than that. His stupidity is cruel. Cruel in an obvious and typical way to Anne: but cruel also to Mrs Clay who, as Anne reflects, is not distinguishable as a widow of about thirty with a common name from the actually socially superior Mrs Smith. Cruel too in its dismissal of friendship and charity as motives. And, finally, even pathetic when the reader reflects on the declined circumstances ('paltry rooms' compared with Kellynch) of Sir Walter himself, and on his ludicrous inflation of the dull Lady Dalrymple and her 'plain and awkward' daughter into the 'nobility of England and Ireland'. Here a class distinction is used by Jane Austen to dramatize far more than class distinctions.

Much the same may be said of episodes all through Jane Austen's work. Elizabeth Bennet's great pivotal assertion of her spirit and intelligence in *Pride and Prejudice* is made, again in an atmosphere of significant comedy, through a point of class. Faced with the majestic and selfish – 'Miss Bennet, do you know who I am?' – demand by Lady Catherine De Bourgh that she should abandon all thoughts of her (infinitely superior) nephew, Elizabeth intrepidly replies: 'He is a gentleman; I am a gentleman's daughter: so far we are equal' (Chapter 56). This is only a truth with some omissions. But it wins the day and wins Mr Darcy.

Even more famous is the irruption of the badly born and bred Mrs Elton into the society of Highbury of which Emma, with some reason, thinks herself the queen. Here a heroine who securely looks down and patronizes is faced with a vulgarian who insists, in a spate of pretensions, on being her immediate equal or superior. The whole of Chapter 32 should be re-read to appreciate the fine fury of their initial encounter. But the following will remind the reader of the flavour:

'And who do you think came in while we were there?'
Emma was quite at a loss. The tone implied some old acquaintance – and how could she possibly guess?
'Knightley!' continued Mrs Elton; – 'Knightley himself! – was not it lucky? – for,

not being within when he called the other day, I had never seen him before; and of course, as so particular a friend of Mr E.'s, I had a great curiosity. "My friend Knightley" had been so often mentioned, that I was really impatient to see him; but I must do my caro sposo the justice to say that he need not be ashamed of his friend. Knightley is quite the gentleman. I like him very much. Decidedly, I think, a very gentleman-like man.'

Happily it was now time to be gone. They were off; and Emma could breathe.

'Insufferable woman!' was her immediate exclamation. 'Worse than I had supposed. Absolutely insufferable! Knightley! – I could not have believed it. Knightley! – never seen him in her life before, and call him Knightley! – and discover that he is a gentleman!'

Here we have two different kinds of snob at war – though clearly at this point Emma is perfectly in the right. And again the system of class is exploited by Jane Austen for further purposes: to embody a crude, stupid ambition coupled with a disregard for language and people, in conflict with offended pride and a proper sense of personal value – in this case that of Mr Knightley.

2 'Miss Austen'

It is now appropriate to comment more thoroughly on the effect that the idea of Jane Austen has upon the reading of her books. By 'idea' I mean the impression of the author, partly as author, partly as historical personality, which we inherit willy-nilly from our background. The most prominent feature of such an impression is its inaccuracy. The more we gain of first-hand acquaintance with an author the more the idea fades. Only crude and banal people are much like the impressions we form of them from casual gossip. And authors who continue to be read are, at least in their writings, far from crude and banal. The images which burden them are generally based on the distortion of a few soap opera characteristics. They are a tribute to our love for cheap anecdote and bad dramatization. In this they probably differ little from the pictures we have of other historical notables: Napoleon was a thin man for most of his life and rarely stuck his arm in his coat; Richard III seems not to have been a hunchback and was obviously no more horrible and wicked than was appropriate to his position – and so on. The difference is that authors can answer back through their works. The pictures of Milton as a disagreeable old 'Puritan'; of Pope as a tedious and sarcastic person who could only think in couplets and always wore a powdered wig; of D. H. Lawrence as the strident and sandalled 'prophet of sex' – all fade and wither when we bother to read not just *about* them but to read them. The only snag is that most people do not bother to read (or cannot) and this makes other people indignant.

But why make a fuss if the question is so trivial? Because, though the question is trivial, the images remain powerful. So powerful that it is not only easy but almost inevitable that the enlightened reader, with the staling of time and the fading of memory, lapses back into the clichés with which he had become so indignant. Perhaps this is why he becomes even more indignant a second time round. And, as I have hinted, the idea of Jane Austen is, for some reason, an exceptionally powerful one.

Why some ideas of this sort are more powerful than others is a mystery. For one thing it seems to depend very little on how *much* we know about an author's life. Five very long, detailed, and rather dull volumes have been written recently about the outwardly uneventful career of Henry James (and there is even another hefty volume devoted to what his contemporaries thought of him); yet few people, even among his enthusiastic readers, appear to have a strong impression of him as a person. About the life of Shakespeare we know almost nothing: yet even the illiterate have some idea of him as a towering genius. In the case of Lord Byron an impression – of the brooding, dangerous, amorous, reckless, revolutionary, despotic, aristocratic whirlwind – seems to have virtually superseded the real man and poet, fascinating though he is. That this is not simply a matter of drama or of public relations is shown by the fact that Jane Austen, about whose quiet life we know so little, is often in danger of sharing Byron's fate. It is a common complaint that even the best and most alert readers have positively to fight against the smothering notion of a cosy and genteel 'Miss Austen'. This would almost seem to demonstrate that it is a true image – that is, until we read (or re-read) her intelligently. Certainly D. H. Lawrence, a critic of genius among other things, did not escape when he wrote in 'À Propos of *Lady Chatterley's Lover*':

> Already this old maid typifies 'personality' instead of character, the sharp knowing in apartness instead of knowing in togetherness, and she is, to my feeling, thoroughly unpleasant, English in the bad, mean, snobbish sense of the word, just as Fielding is English in the good, generous sense. *(Phoenix* II)

Lawrence's violence has some excuse, for he was defending himself against vicious persecution. The same can hardly be said of Henry James, another great critic and novelist and furthermore in some ways a literary descendant of hers, when, scornfully aware of the current 'pleasant twaddle' about the '"dear", our dear, everybody's dear Jane', he nevertheless goes on to talk of:

... The extraordinary grace of her facility, in fact of her unconsciousness: as if, at the most, for difficulty, for embarrassment, she sometimes, over the work basket, her tapestry flowers, in the spare, cool drawing-room of other days, fell a-musing, lapsed too metaphorically, as one may say, into wool gathering, and her dropped stitches, of these pardonable, of these precious moments, were afterwards picked up as little touches of human truth, little glimpses of steady vision, little master strokes of imagination.   ('The Lesson of Balzac', 1905)

This seems *little* indeed. Especially when we know that James was aware that Lord Macaulay, whom he wittily but rather lethally calls her 'first slightly ponderous *amoroso*' (people in glass houses . . .?) had written in 1843 that he had 'no hesitation in placing Jane Austen, a woman of whom England is justly proud' as near to Shakespeare in the truth of her characterization.

This is perhaps enough to prove the point that the 'Jane' idea is dangerous. But since part of the present subject is *Persuasion*, it is appropriate to mention finally the curious attitude evinced by yet another distinguished writer. As an epilogue to his (rather inferior) 'Cockney' short story about a club of Jane Austen fanatics in the trenches in the First World War, appropriately called 'The Janeites', Kipling tags on a little poem which is beautifully illustrative of the terrible complications that abound. Jane Austen goes to Paradise; is greeted by no less than Scott, Fielding, Smollett, Cervantes and Shakespeare; is offered 'anything in Heaven's gift' by the Archangels: chooses 'Love'; then:

> In a private limbo
> Where none had thought to look,
> Sat a Hampshire gentleman
> Reading of a book.
> It was called *Persuasion*,
> And it told the plain
> Story of the love between
> Him and Jane.
>
> He heard the question
> Circle Heaven through –
> Closed the book and answered:
> 'I did – and do!'
> Quietly but speedily
> (As Captain Wentworth moved)
> Entered into Paradise
> The man Jane loved!

No wonder *we* become confused.

3   Literary Predecessors

Henry James wrote of 'her unconsciousness'. If this was meant to mean that Jane Austen had no idea of what she was doing in writing novels, it is a compliment in the same fanciful class as Milton's celebrated reference, in 'L'Allegro', to Shakespeare warbling 'his native Wood-notes wilde'. We know that she read very widely in past and contemporary literature, and just as Shakespeare provides a brilliant discourse on art and nature in *Hamlet*, Jane Austen uncharacteristically addresses the reader directly in *Northanger Abbey*:

... I will not adopt that ungenerous and impolitic custom so common among novel writers, of degrading by their contemptuous censure the very performances, to the number of which they are themselves adding – joining with their greatest enemies in bestowing the harshest epithets on such works, and scarcely ever permitting them to be read by their own heroine, who, if she accidentally take up a novel, is sure to turn over its insipid pages with disgust. Alas! if the heroine of one novel be not patronized by the heroine of another, from whom can she expect protection and regard? I cannot approve of it ... There seems almost a general wish of decrying the capacity and undervaluing the labour of the novelist, and of slighting the performances which have only genius, wit, and taste to recommend them. 'I am no novel reader – I seldom look into novels – Do not imagine that *I* often read novels – It is really very well for a novel.' – Such is the common cant. – 'And what are you reading Miss —?' 'Oh! it is only a novel!' replies the young lady; while she lays down her book with affected indifference, or momentary shame. – 'It is only Cecilia, or Camilla, or Belinda;' or, in short, only some work in which the greatest powers of the mind are displayed, in which the most thorough knowledge of human nature, the happiest delineation of its varieties, the liveliest effusions of wit and humour are conveyed to the world in the best chosen language.   (Chapter 5)

I should think that the warmth of this – humorous though it is – is partly accounted for by the fact that the novel was, relatively, a new form; and that Jane Austen was conscious of having brought it to a new perfection. In the eighteenth century, broadly speaking, the novel had two enemies: poetry and lies. Poetry was accounted (and the attitude lingers on) the highest type of literature. Indeed it is easy to imagine Jane Austen being daunted by the compact brilliance and penetration in her own field – satirical observation of marriage customs – by this kind of thing from Pope:

> The Gods, to curse *Pamela* with her Pray'rs,
> Gave the gilt Coach and dappled *Flanders* Mares,
> The shining Robes, rich Jewels, Beds of State,
> And to compleat her Bliss, a Fool for Mate.
> She glares in *Balls*, Front-boxes, and the *Ring*,

> A vain, unquiet, glitt'ring, wretched Thing!
> Pride, Pomp, and State but reach her outward Part,
> She sighs, and is no *Dutchess* at her Heart.

('Epistle to Miss Blount, With the Works of Voiture', 1711)

Poetry was Art. And capable, too, of the sublime. Whereas prose was the medium of ordinary communication, at its highest when conveying moral, philosophical, theological, or historical truth. It is highly instructive to note that Charles Darwin's grandfather, Erasmus, wrote his great scientific treatise *The Botanic Garden* (1789–91) in heroic couplets. But it is even more instructive that the early novelists clearly felt obliged to justify their practice by more or less elaborate, though increasingly tongue-in-cheek, stratagems. The word fiction even now has its dark side – 'That is a pure fiction.' And, really, how could one justify wasting people's time – and possibly corrupting their morals – with tales of irreligious, lecherous and violent people who did not even exist? With lies? Of course, this is something of a caricature of current attitudes: eighteenth-century educated people were certainly not less intelligent, though they may have been more serious, than people today. But we should bear in mind that the growing audience for prose fiction had in it in very large proportion that newly prosperous, newly literate, and newly respectable part of society which comes under the perplexed term 'middle class' and which presumably, like most audiences, wanted to hear its own values and practices praised at the same time as being amused. The literary evidence certainly seems to bear this out. Prefaces or disquisitions in the text, like the following, are choc-a-bloc in the period:

If I have not succeeded in my endeavours to unfold the mysteries of fraud, to instruct the ignorant, and entertain the vacant; if I have failed in my attempts to subject folly to ridicule, and vice to indignation; to arouse the spirit of mirth, wake the soul of compassion, and touch the secret springs that move the heart; I have, at least, adorned virtue with honour and applause, branded iniquity with reproach and shame, and carefully avoided every hint or expression which could give umbrage to the most delicate reader ...

This is Smollett's description, not of a sermon, but of his racy novel, *The Adventures of Ferdinand Count Fathom* (1753). But things went deeper than mere assertion. Defoe, for example, that 'false, shuffling, prevaricating rascal' or prolific genius and 'father of the novel' (according to taste), constantly felt inclined or obliged to present his fictions as *true*. *Robinson Crusoe* (1720) was based on the experiences of the famous and eccentric castaway Alexander Selkirk. It claims to be 'a just history of fact; neither is there any appearance of fiction in it'. Even more strikingly, *A*

Journal of the Plague Year (1722) purports to be and sounds like the true, unvarnished account of the Great Plague of London of 1665:

> It was about the beginning of September, 1664, that I, among the rest of my neighbours, heard, in ordinary discourse, that the plague was returned again in Holland . . .

From this sober beginning the horror of the constantly encroaching epidemic is evoked by the unsparing accumulation of seemingly factual detail; not the least effective part of which is the use of lists and statistical tables.

That Jane Austen had absolutely no desire or need for such devices or for self-justification is striking in context. Her fiction is unashamedly fiction. But we should note that the pretence of factuality continued and still continues. It has become a literary convention with its own uses. Henry James, for example, clearly had no need to establish his factual credentials as Defoe did. But in his most famous ghost story, *The Turn of the Screw* (1898), he prefaces the main action by a little scene in which the narrator listens to a friend's reading of a manuscript written by the latter's late governess, of which an 'exact transcription of my own' forms the main story. This elaboration has its own peculiar purposes, irrelevant here. But every reader will recognize the device.

To return to the eighteenth century. The two dominant English novelists of the mid century were Fielding and Richardson. They were, and are, commonly thought of as rivals – indeed Fielding started as a novelist by writing an extremely funny burlesque of Richardson's *Pamela* (1741–2) called *Shamela*; and the general difference between them was decisively remarked upon by Dr Johnson 'as between a man who knew how a watch was made [Richardson], and a man who could tell the hour by looking on the dial-plate [Fielding]' – in which he oddly echoes an earlier remark of Richardson's to Fielding's sister. But what they had in common was their misgivings about presenting fiction without explanation. Fielding tackled the problem in *Tom Jones* (1749) by claiming, as 'the founder of a new province of writing', to be writing a 'History' which is superior to 'all the romances, novels, plays, and poems, with which the stalls abound'. He writes as though this were actually the case, beginning the story with: 'In . . . Somersetshire, there lately lived, *and perhaps lives still*, a gentleman whose name was Allworthy . . .' (my italics), although it would need a stupid reader to take him at face value – especially when confronted with a good squire called Allworthy. Earlier, in *Joseph Andrews* (1742), he had concocted a definition of his kind of fiction as a 'comic epic poem in prose'. This humorous elaboration is certainly preferable to the 'moral' protestations of the kind quoted from Smollett.

But the important point here is still that an explanation was felt to be necessary even from so lordly and self-confident a writer as Fielding.

Richardson's answer to the problem was different and extremely influential. If not the first, he was certainly the greatest writer of the novel in letters, the 'epistolary' novel. This form has obvious and subtle advantages in its capacity to create dramatic interaction, to describe the same event from differing points of view, to reveal the intimate workings of the mind, and so on. It was copied all over Europe and inspired some of the greatest novelists of the age (Laclos in France and Goethe in Weimar, for example). Jane Austen herself experimented with it and parodied it in her very earliest writings, and remained a devotee of Richardson, as were Fanny Burney and Maria Edgeworth who she selects for admiration in *Northanger Abbey*. She is supposed to have known his *Sir Charles Grandison* (1753–4) almost by heart; and the reader of *Persuasion* may note the importance of letters near the end of the book. But it also has disadvantages. Fielding's dislike of the device finds justification in such absurdities as people living in the same house constantly communicating by letter; and as Johnson (again) remarked, 'if you were to read Richardson for the story, your impatience would be so much fretted that you would hang yourself'. Diderot agreed. It is therefore interesting, though not surprising, that this elaborate mode of composition had its origins closer to life than to art. Richardson was asked to write letters for the use of 'those country readers who are unable to indite for themselves':

> Will it be any harm, said I, in a piece you want written so low, if we should instruct them how they should think & act in common cases, as well as indite? . . . I set about it, & in the progress of it, writing two or three letters to instruct handsome girls, who were obliged to go out to service, as we phrase it, how to avoid the snares that might be laid against their virtue; the above story recurred to my thought; and hence sprung Pamela.

Even in his masterpiece *Clarissa* (1747–8), Richardson, besieged as he was by lady readers anxious that he keep the virtuous heroine alive, maintains in great and painstaking detail the transparent pretence that the letters are 'real'. Such was the force of the convention.

Knowledge of such previous needs and their results is not, of course, essential to reading Jane Austen – or anyone else – intelligently. Logically everyone has to start somewhere. But it can enhance our understanding. It can enable us to see the truth in the commonly held judgement (commonly held, at any rate, since the publication of F. R. Leavis's *The Great Tradition* in 1948) that Jane Austen's works are a kind of focal point in the English novel: originating a new way of writing while drawing on and, as it were, summing up her predecessors. Not that she herself particularly welcomed discussion of such 'technical' matters. One of her very few surviving comments on her methods is a humorous passing remark to Cassandra on the reactions of their sixteen-year-old niece, Fanny Knight:

> I am gratified by her having pleasure in what I write – but I wish the knowledge of my being exposed to her discerning Criticism, may not hurt my stile, by inducing too great a solicitude. I begin already to weigh my words and sentences more than I did, and I am looking about for a sentiment, an illustration or a metaphor in every corner of the room. Could my Ideas flow as fast as the rain in the Store closet it would be charming.   (*Letters*, page 256)

Note the metaphor. But her mastery of expression is evident in all her work. Consider, as an example, her handling of narration. The normal way for a novelist to tell a story is through what is called the 'omniscient narrator'. This is also the normal way to tell a story in life: 'There was a man who had a dog called Fido who was always running away . . . , etc.' Jane Austen uses it. But so do many other writers. The difference lies in the quality and economy of her use. Here is the opening of a story by the currently popular author Jeffrey Archer:

> Sir Hamish Graham had many of the qualities and most of the failings that result from being born to a middle-class Scottish family. He was well educated, hard working and honest, while at the same time being narrow-minded, uncompromising and proud. Never on any occasion had he allowed hard liquor to pass his lips, and he mistrusted all men who had not been born north of Hadrian's Wall and many of those who had.

This certainly leads one into the story. But if the reader pauses at all it will surely be to wonder at the number of clichés it contains. Here is a comedian's Scotsman presented with apparent seriousness. Compare:

> It is a truth universally acknowledged, that a single man in possession of a good fortune, must be in want of a wife.

Pride and Prejudice also opens with a cliché. But it is subjected to ridicule in the very act of statement. This is obvious enough, and I am not suggesting that the comparison is really fair to Mr Archer. What it does is to indicate the wit and control of tone found in Jane Austen. Consider a much longer example from *Pride and Prejudice*: the heroine, believing herself embarrassingly at odds with her former suitor, the aristocratic Mr Darcy, suddenly learns that the plans and destination of a tour with her aunt and uncle have been changed:

> With the mention of Derbyshire, there were many ideas connected. It was impossible for her to see the word without thinking of Pemberley and its owner. 'But surely,' said she, 'I may enter his county with impunity, and rob it of a few petrified spars without his perceiving me.'

The period of expectation was now doubled. Four weeks were to pass away before her uncle and aunt's arrival. But they did pass away, and Mr and Mrs Gardiner, with their four children, did at length arrive at Longbourn ... The Gardiners staid only one night ... and set off the next morning with Elizabeth in pursuit of novelty and amusement ... It is not the object of this work to give a description of Derbyshire, nor of any of the remarkable places through which their route thither lay; Oxford, Blenheim, Warwick, Kenelworth, Birmingham, &c. are sufficiently known. A small part of Derbyshire is all the present concern. To the little town of Lambton, the scene of Mrs Gardiner's former residence, and where she had lately learned that some acquaintance still remained, they bent their steps, after having seen all the principal wonders of the country; and within five miles of Lambton, Elizabeth found from her aunt, that Pemberley was situated. It was not in their direct road, nor more than a mile or two out of it. In talking over their route the evening before, Mrs Gardiner expressed an inclination to see the place again. Mr Gardiner declared his willingness, and Elizabeth was applied to for her approbation.

'My love, should not you like to see a place of which you have heard so much?' said her aunt. 'A place too, with which so many of your acquaintances are connected. Wickham passed all his youth there, you know.'

Elizabeth was distressed. She felt that she had no business at Pemberley, and was obliged to assume a disinclination for seeing it. She must own that she was tired of great houses; after going over so many, she really had no pleasure in fine carpets or satin curtains.

Mrs Gardiner abused her stupidity. 'If it were merely a fine house richly furnished,' said she, 'I should not care about it myself; but the grounds are delightful. They have some of the finest woods in the country.'

Elizabeth said no more – but her mind could not acquiesce. The possibility of meeting Mr Darcy, while viewing the place, instantly occurred. It would be dreadful! She blushed at the very idea; and thought it would be better to speak openly to her aunt, than to run such a risk. But against this, there were objections; and she finally resolved that it could be the last resource, if her private enquiries as to the absence of the family, were unfavourably answered.

Accordingly, when she retired at night, she asked the chambermaid whether Pemberley were not a very fine place, what was the name of its proprietor, and with no little alarm, whether the family were down for the summer. A most welcome negative followed the last question – and her alarms being now removed, she was at leisure to feel a great deal of curiosity to see the house herself; and when the subject was revived the next morning, and she was again applied to, could readily answer, and with a proper air of indifference, that she had not really any dislike to the scheme.

To Pemberley, therefore, they were to go.   (Chapter 42)

This is a good, but not especially remarkable, passage of Jane Austen and one's first reaction might well be that it rounds off the volume with aplomb and excites anticipation for what is to follow – which it does. But a closer analysis reveals a whole complex of devices, part of the point of which is that they do not draw undue attention to themselves. For example, in the third sentence the 'said she' is deceptive: Elizabeth is not addressing anyone aloud. She is thinking. But her thoughts are not the hardly verbalized impulses and making of connections which constitute 'real' everyday thought. When people report having 'said to themselves', I doubt very much whether words are always used (this is a matter of controversy among philosophers) – and certainly not used in the elegant and witty manner of Elizabeth with her 'petrified spars'. Our attention is still focused on her, in a more generalized way, in the next sentence: it is *her* 'expectation' we are concerned with. But there follows a mere narrator's statement of fact even if the choice of 'pass away' suggests waiting rather than enjoying. That it might do so is suggested by the repetition of the phrase as we turn back into Elizabeth's mind in the next sentence with its emphatic 'did ... did'. So even in this apparently functional little passage Jane Austen can be seen to be positively packing in suggestion and nuance.

Of course, nobody normally reads with this kind of plodding attention. But the general effect of brilliance surely depends on such lively detail being at least semi-consciously noticed.

The following paragraph is entirely concerned with moving the action on in a direct narration which artfully describes the journey, while denying any such aim. 'Bent their steps' is a deliberately ordinary metaphor, I think. But now we meet Jane Austen's mastery of psychological manoeuvre in an intensified form. Mrs Gardiner's directly reported suggestion is unintentionally very painful to Elizabeth who must all the time be thinking that she might have been mistress of the great house, and cannot but be humiliated by the innocent reminder of the caddish Wickham whose bogus claims she had ignorantly supported against Mr Darcy. The author points this out in a neutral tone – but then suddenly switches to a different kind of presentation. 'She must own that she was tired ...' is not the author's voice, but Elizabeth's, this time *indirectly* reported. Back, in the next paragraph, to Mrs Gardiner. Then to Elizabeth, but with an entirely new device. 'It would be dreadful!' is not the narrator, not direct speech to others, not free indirect speech, not 'saying to oneself' but a catching at the thought at the moment it occurs, a kind of small drama of the mind. Then, through the middle ground of 'She blushed ...' back to a description of thoughts as opposed to dramatization. And so on – until the provoking final sentence.

No wonder Jane Austen is so much admired. For the 'light, and bright and sparkling' nature of *Pride and Prejudice* is the result of an unobtrusive but absolute control which makes much of the work of her predecessors seem like well-intentioned blundering.

*

The defence of novels in Chapter 5 of *Northanger Abbey* goes on to contrast their failure to be respectable with the success of another form:

> Now, had the same young lady been engaged with a volume of the Spectator ... how proudly would she have produced the book, and told its name; though the chances must be against her being occupied by any part of that voluminous publication, of which either the matter or manner would not disgust a young person of taste ...

That this is an odd judgement in many ways is, I think, not enough noticed. For one thing it is very much in the balanced judgemental manner of the publication attacked and its successors – the periodical essay being one of the main, and sometimes great, literary forms of the eighteenth century which has since then suffered an uninterrupted decline into its present negligibility, its functions being taken over appropriately enough by the novel. And, more importantly, we know of Jane Austen's wide reading in the form, and, in particular, of 'my dear Dr Johnson'. The avowed object of the *Spectator* under Addison and Steele (1711–14) was to 'enliven morality with wit, and to temper wit with morality'; and although this patronizing description may make the modern reader wilt a little, something like it is certainly achieved in the most decisive and glittering fashion by Johnson in his various writings. Particularly to the point here is that the direction taken by the pursuit of 'morality' – i.e. observations on the human predicament – is the creation of examples; examples, to be convincing, become little stories; and little stories in the hands of genius have a tendency to grow beyond their original purpose. In Johnson's case they grew, one could say, into the major achievement of *Rasselas: Prince of Abyssinia* (1759), a moral entertainment in the form of a kind of 'novel' whose brilliance is matched only in Voltaire's *Candide* (also 1759), and its profundity almost nowhere. (It is also no surprise that Richardson wrote for Johnson's *Rambler*.) However that may be, the tradition of prose moralizing as well as that of the novel *per se* was clearly very much present to Jane Austen; and her punishment of the *Spectator* might be seen not only as a defence of her own medium against those likely to demand 'and what are you reading, Miss—?' but also as a precursor of Anne Elliot's less amused but equally firm response to Captain Harville during the climax of *Persuasion*:

> 'Yes, yes if you please, no reference to examples in books. Men have had every advantage of us in telling their own story. Education has been theirs in so much higher a degree; the pen has been in their hands. I will not allow books to prove any thing.' (Chapter 23)

In no other great creative art do women so closely challenge or surpass men as in writing novels – a truth so clear as to be usually ignored or forgotten.

There is little reason, for the present purpose, to say much more about Jane Austen's reading. The poet Cowper was a great favourite, often alluded to in the novels. So was Crabbe, whom she jokingly wished to 'comfort' on hearing of the death of his wife in 1813, and who, in that complex age of novels and 'Romanticism', wrote extraordinarily fine short stories in eighteenth-century couplets. Finally – and mainly relevant here to *Persuasion* – it is impossible to ignore the presence of the Gothick/Romantic element in contemporary literary culture. That the two were linked may easily be suggested by mentioning Coleridge's authorship of 'The Rime of the Ancient Mariner'. The best short introduction to Gothick novels and their essential spirit is, of course, *Northanger Abbey* itself. But it should be added that Mrs Radcliffe, who is affectionately satirized there, far from being merely the writer of the sensational trash of our current estimate, is quite capable of Austen-like ironies and deflations: 'But hark!' says Emily, the heroine of *Mysteries of Udolpho* (1794), to her father,

'here comes the sweeping sound over the wood-tops – Now it dies away. How solemn the stillness that succeeds! Now the breeze swells again! It is like the voice of some supernatural being – the voice of the spirit of the woods, that watches over them by night. Ah! What light is yonder? But it is gone! And now it gleams again, near the root of that large chestnut: look, sir!'

'Are you such an admirer of nature,' said St Aubert, 'and so little acquainted with her appearances, as not to know that for the glow-worm?'

This may remind us of the treatment of Marianne Dashwood's effusions on the beauties of nature in *Sense and Sensibility*; that in turn of Jane Austen's deep and constant concern with the relation between depth of feeling and ease of feeling; and that in turn of Captain Benwick's admiration for Scott and Byron. Of which more later.

II Emma

Nobody who has read a story really needs a commentator – a drudge – to tell it to him again in less well chosen language. In life an anecdote is usually more interesting in what it says about the narrator than about what is narrated – hence the frequent inability to remember exactly what it was that someone was so funny about. And in highly accomplished and clear narratives like *Emma* and *Persuasion* the sequence of events can easily be checked, while the interest lies in what they dramatize, imply, and mean. I shall therefore abandon the tedious practice of going through the novels as it were chronologically. Instead I shall talk first about Jane Austen's methods and the kind of creative control she exercises over her materials (sections 1 and 2). Then, on the basis of and arising from this discussion, I shall talk about how these materials become high art in a comic drama of vital issues as opposed to sublimated gossip (sections 3, 4 and 5). *Persuasion* will be similarly treated. It seems a less chore-like activity all round. But it is as well to start at the beginning, as you will see.

1 Chapter 1

Emma, elegant, witty, and rich in meaning, with a finely adapted form and a comic tone, unites some of the best blessings of the novel; and it has existed since December 1815 with very few to dislike it or disturb its reputation.

It is, however, one thing to utter pleasant generalities about this book, and quite another to justify these in detail. Let us consider the opening:

> Emma Woodhouse, handsome, clever, and rich, with a comfortable home and happy disposition, seemed to unite some of the best blessings of existence; and had lived nearly twenty-one years in the world with very little to distress or vex her.

This paragraph plunges us directly into the subject. It invites quick and easy reading, partly because it is a single sentence. It promises a happy and attractive subject. Nobody could take it as the opening of a tragedy. There is no tedious elaboration or scene setting to allow the mind to wander, or to wonder when the real story is going to start. It is not self-consciously learned or allusive. And so on. Yet all this plain sailing is qualified by one word which is to be crucial to the development of the action and the meaning of the book: 'seemed'. Emma's advantages only potentially confer the best blessings of existence on her – as is obvious if we consider the question.

The second paragraph extends the effect. It is similarly crisp, informative and subtle. In the major key, as it were, we learn of Emma's 'affectionate' father; her being mistress of the house, and of her excellent and loving governess. In the minor key we are told that her father is 'indulgent'; her mother long dead; and her governess 'short' of a mother in affection (though only a little). The attentive reader begins to learn Jane Austen's refined art of qualification.

The third paragraph leans slightly more towards the adverse. Miss Taylor's loving excellence had resulted in only nominal authority; she has imposed hardly any restraint; and Emma does what she likes. It comes as no surprise, therefore, that the fourth paragraph starts by dropping the hitherto apparently neutral stance of the narrator. 'The real evils indeed of Emma's situation were the power of having rather too much her own way, and a disposition to think a little too well of herself ...' There is no seeming here: the 'evils' are 'real' and emphatic ('indeed'). Are we then, contrary to the expectations excited by the opening, in for some moralizing piece about how awful it is to be handsome, clever, and rich? Obviously not, for – and this is what we may well call Art – the qualifications join the opposing team: 'rather too much', 'a little too well'. The happiness begins to reassert itself.

In a very few words Jane Austen has not only stated her subject, but alerted us as to how to read about it. She now proceeds to expand both her subject and her method. In the remainder of Chapter 1 the first stress seems relatively unimportant at the time, but is in fact crucial. Emma lives in a desperately dull society, and it is in this context that we must see her impetuous and high-handed actions. 'Highbury ... afforded her no equals': this states a satisfying social eminence, but it also suggests a demoralizing tedium – which the author probably knew a great deal about. Highbury is very real; and not as the eminent American critic Lionel Trilling once suggested, a kind of 'pastoral' English backcloth.

The first *action* is that of Mr Woodhouse composing himself for his 'sleep after dinner, as usual' – a prelude to the first of their seemingly endless 'long' evenings together. The attitude of both daughter and author to Mr Woodhouse repays examination. They have a similarly unsentimental view of him. The author informs us succinctly that he had been 'a valetudinarian all his life, without activity of mind or body ... and though everywhere beloved for the friendliness of his heart and his amiable temper, his talents could not have recommended him at any time'. Emma recognizes this: 'She dearly loved her father, but he was no companion for her. He could not meet her in conversation, rational or playful', but, most remarkably, her love is not simply felt as a duty (as that of the overtly more tender Anne Elliot for *her* father must be) but is an active principle which rules this critical and headstrong girl throughout the novel. Typically, Jane Austen immediately develops this situation in relation to a second stressed concern, marriage; equally typically, her description is focused and 'proved' by the dramatization afforded by dialogue. The conversation beginning: 'Poor Miss Taylor! – I wish she were here again. What a pity it is that Mr Weston ever thought of her!' is, of course, comic – which is just as well, for with a different tone Mr Woodhouse's ludicrous worries about James and the 'poor horses' would seem a biting demonstration of silly egotism. Particularly revealing is his stifling inability to see any reason for a newly married woman having 'a house of her own'. Since Emma's skilful 'exertions' merely steer him round towards a happier end of the evening, we are left with the question as to whether she is right to be so indulgent. And, as if to determine this, 'Mr Knightley, a sensible man about seven or eight-and-thirty', steps in with the dramatic appropriateness that the reader (after four pages) is learning to expect. He quickly earns his right to be called sensible – i.e. both feeling and rational – by the cordial tact with which he handles Mr Woodhouse's hypochondriacal worries and by his pleasant settling of the issue of Mrs Weston: '... but when it comes to the question of dependence or independence! ...'

Jane Austen almost always creates her characters most deeply through their speech. It is significant, therefore, that Mr Knightley's place in Emma's world is shown almost entirely, as the chapter concludes, through his part in the discussion. And the discussion itself very naturally still concerns the proprieties of marriage. There are three voices. Mr Woodhouse is plaintively against the whole business, and therefore against match-making. But his fussings against fuss are affectionately ignored. Emma, so rational hitherto, babbles gaily and imprudently on:

'... Pray do not make any more matches.'

'I promise you to make none for myself, papa; but I must, indeed, for other people. It is the greatest amusement in the world! And after such success you know! – Every body said that Mr Weston would never marry again ... All manner of solemn nonsense was talked on the subject, but I believed none of it. Ever since the day (about four years ago) that Miss Taylor and I met with him in Broadway-lane, when, because it began to mizzle, he darted away with so much gallantry, and borrowed two umbrellas for us from Farmer Mitchell's, I made up my mind on the subject. I planned the match from that hour; and when such success has blessed me in this instance, dear papa, you cannot think that I shall leave off match-making.'

The mizzling in Broadway-lane and Farmer Mitchell's two umbrellas are irrelevant details of the kind Emma is later to despise in the verbal torrents of Miss Bates. But the triumphant egotism is, unfortunately, all her own, and gives its first substance to the 'disposition to think a little too well of herself' of which we have heard. Mr Knightley's reply is an entirely different register:

> 'I do not understand what you mean by "success" ... Success supposes endeavour. Your time has been properly and delicately spent, if you have been endeavouring for the last four years to bring about this marriage. A worthy employment for a young lady's mind! But if, which I rather imagine, your making the match as you call it, means only your planning it, your saying to yourself one idle day, "I think it would be a very good thing for Miss Taylor if Mr Weston were to marry her," and saying it again to yourself every now and then afterwards, – why do you talk of success? where is your merit? – what are you proud of? – you made a lucky guess; and *that* is all that can be said.'

This is entirely logical; trenchant without being pompous; and firm without being domineering. Mr Knightley is shown to be a source of good judgement, and shown by the force of his argument rather than by the kind of automatic pious correctness we often associate with 'good' heroes. But, again, if the reader is nevertheless put off by such virtue at such an early stage, he must be relieved by the completely unabashed gaiety of Emma's retort. And so the argument goes good-humouredly on. The chapter closes with the introduction of the subject of Mr Elton. But as the first words were about Emma, so the last belong to Mr Knightley:

> '... help him to the best of the fish and the chicken, but leave him to chuse his own wife. Depend upon it, a man of six or seven-and-twenty can take care of himself.'

I have spent some time upon this chapter because only a consideration of detail can demonstrate the types of perfection offered by *Emma*. Jane Austen has occasionally been called a 'poet'. Leaving aside the question of verse, this seemingly bizarre description is appropriate if what we expect of poetry is that every (or nearly every) word has a place in the creation of a significant fiction. Can the reader find anything either dull or superfluous in the chapter? It would be interesting if he could.

Before going on to the more substantial interests of the novel I shall try to confirm the present discussion by looking at Chapter 12 in which we see how exciting and entertaining the commonplace can become under intensive treatment. It is a dangerous little drama of trivia.

2 'What mighty Contests rise from trivial Things' (Pope)

Chapter 12 is a piece of gruesome domestic comedy. The harmony between Emma and Mr Knightley has been broken by his severe disapproval of her intervention between Harriet and Robert Martin. The general harmony is threatened by the bringing together of so many established prejudices and foibles. The occasion of discord is, very naturally, a family dinner. And the first passage therefore repairs the alliance of good sense and good feeling between Emma and Mr Knightley, her deviations from which constitute the main action of both chapter *and* book. After an exchange of affectionate sarcasms they make concessions (not capitulations) and are reconciled:

'... I only want to know that Mr Martin is not very, very bitterly disappointed.'
  'A man cannot be more so,' was his short, full answer.
  'Ah! – Indeed I am very sorry. – Come shake hands with me.'

We are now free, as it were, to look round the room. John Knightley's entrance occasions a direct authorial comment of a kind unusual in Jane Austen:

'How d'ye do, George?' and 'John, how are you?' succeeded in the true English style, burying under a calmness that seemed all but indifference, the real attachment which would have led either of them, if requisite, to do every thing for the good of the other.

This is gratifying to the patriot, and stands out from its context because it is a generalization about the state of society. (Perhaps the war with France is remotely in the background.) But the dramatized Englishness which follows is of a more familiar kind. The conversation is about the weather; the children; common ailments and what respective medical oracles have to say about them; the merits of holiday resorts and different kinds of air, and so on. The exception to this is the businesslike talk indicated in the background about 'the plan of a drain, the change of a fence, the felling of a tree, and the destination of every acre for wheat, turnips, or spring corn ...', etc., but this is significantly conducted between the two Mr Knightleys. Emma hovers like an anxious impresario in between, and she is rightly anxious because the assorted crotchets are bound to clash. At first things are easy, 'quiet and conversible'. Even Mr Woodhouse's gruel – a potential danger – is obtained without difficulty:

'... My dear Emma, suppose we all have a little gruel.'
  Emma could not suppose any such thing, knowing, as she did, that both the Mr Knightleys were as unpersuadable on that article as herself; – and two basins only were ordered.

But immediately the two absent physicians, Perry and Wingfield, join in proxy battle on the question of sea and sea air. 'Mr Wingfield most strenuously recommended it, sir,' says Isabella Knightley to her father. 'Ah! my dear, but Perry had many doubts about the sea doing ... any good.' Emma has to jump to the rescue, 'feeling this to be an unsafe subject', and direct the conversation towards the question of Perry's own health. Although 'poor Perry is bilious' according to Mr Woodhouse, Isabella sees a way back to her *idée fixe* and promptly takes it: 'He will be so pleased to see my little ones.' But Mr Woodhouse is a match for her and skilfully turns her flank with '... you had better let him look at little Bella's throat'. Isabella falls back on bathing and Wingfield, but this provokes the debile contestants to such relative heat that Emma is forced to use her diversionary tactics again: 'You seem to me to have forgotten Mrs and Miss Bates.' No good; for Isabella quickly offers them the ultimate praise of 'they are always so pleased to see my children'; and reverts to health. She quotes Wingfield as saying that 'colds were never so prevalent as they have been this autumn'. (The great influenza epidemic of 1803 may be in the background here.) Mr Woodhouse retorts with Perry's view that it is 'not ... altogether a sickly season' and his own that London is always unhealthy. Yes, says Isabella, but not in Brunswick Square – Wingfield approves of the air in Brunswick Square. Mr Woodhouse is unshaken: 'Ah! my dear, it is not like Hartfield.' Isabella cannot contradict her father, but 'excepting those little nervous head-aches and palpitations which I am never free from any where' the John Knightley family are all very well. Mr Woodhouse is still not impressed: they are only 'middling' and 'Mr John Knightley very far from looking well'. This last infelicity is going too far and provokes a characteristically brusque response from its subject, who has overheard it and directs his exasperation through his wife: 'Be satisfied with doctoring and coddling yourself and the children, and let me look as I chuse.' This is altogether too vigorous and calls for a correspondingly ambitious, even extravagant, piece of pacification from Emma:

'I did not thoroughly understand what you were telling your brother,' cried Emma, 'about your friend Mr Graham's intending to have a bailiff from Scotland, to look after his new estate. But will it answer? Will not the old prejudice be too strong?'

This is successful. But the ominous reintroduction of gruel, accompanied by 'pretty severe Philippics upon the many houses where it was never met with tolerable', is a prelude to even greater danger. We proceed from the gruel-ignorant servant at South End to Perry versus Wingfield in the guise of Cromer versus South End, and thence inevitably to a second and much more thunderous counter-attack from John Knightley:

'Mr Perry,' said he, in a voice of very strong displeasure, 'would do as well to keep his opinion till it is asked for. Why does he make it any business of his, to wonder at what I do? – At my taking my family to one part of the coast or another?

– I may be allowed, I hope, the use of my judgment as well as Mr Perry. – I want his directions no more than his drugs.'

He softens to a tone of 'only sarcastic dryness', but the damage to family harmony is such that his brother is obliged to support and take over Emma's role. 'True, true,' he cries to John's exposition of the exact mileage from London to Cromer, but then strikes off decisively to 'My idea of moving the path to Langham, of turning it more to the right that it may not cut through the home meadows ...' Explosion is avoided. The chapter ends with an authorial confirmation of what we have probably noticed: that Mr Woodhouse 'had, in fact, though unconsciously, been attributing many of his own feelings and expressions' to Mr Perry. This is valuable in our conceited century which often glibly assumes that knowledge of unconscious behaviour did not exist before the theories of Freud were diffused and defused (an assumption, incidentally, about which Freud himself was appropriately scathing).

Chapter 12, then, demonstrates in miniature the importance of the alliance between Emma and Mr Knightley, as did Chapter 1. It is an alliance of alert sensibility and quick thought; it is characterized by their intuitive grasp of what is right both functionally and, by extension, morally; and it works largely through language. It acts in the context of a more or less comic dullness, self-concern, and meandering in consequentiality which makes up most of the rest of Highbury and, by extension, society as a whole. I shall, of course, be discussing its ups and downs later on. But first a brief confirmatory example. In Chapter 15 the problem of how to get half a mile home from the Westons after a few flakes of snow have fallen causes immense concern. Mr Woodhouse is, of course, completely *bouleversé*; John Knightley triumphs with this chance for a sarcastic vision of disaster; Mrs Weston tries, with Emma, to be of comfort; Mr Weston enthusiastically grasps the opportunity for extending even more unwanted goodwill and hospitality; Isabella is heroically ready to brave the elements in order to get back to her children – and so on. 'What is to be done, my dear Emma? – what is to be done?' exclaims Mr Woodhouse, for, as always, 'to her he looked for comfort'. What is to be done is that Mr Knightley goes out to look at the weather and talk to the coachmen, sees that it offers no inconvenience, let alone threat, and reports. The resolution is as meaningfully precise as the consternation was diffuse:

Mr Knightley and Emma settled it in a few brief sentences: thus –
'Your father will not be easy; why do not you go?'
'I am ready, if the others are.'

'Shall I ring the bell?'
'Yes, do.'
And the bell was rung, and the carriages spoken for.

This clear-headed efficiency amidst varieties of incompetence is a kind of moral pointer in Jane Austen: compare the impression that Anne's behaviour makes on Captain Wentworth after the accident at Lyme in *Persuasion*. But here we note that it is the prelude to Emma's first real disaster, Mr Elton's shocking and shaming proposal of marriage.

These scenes, together with many others, are occasions on which Jane Austen is redressing the balance in favour of her heroine. How *well* Emma comes out of them; and how easy it is to ignore or forget them when expatiating on her bossiness and self-deception. No one should be misled into thinking that because the excitement – the narrow escapes, the clashes, the sailing close to the wrong subjects, the heroic salvation of situations – is made up of trivia, it is therefore trivial. The qualities shown, good or bad, are real and important.

Actually Jane Austen also presents a familiar problem about literature in a particularly nagging form. Chapter 12 (and this is *merely* an example), probably because and not in spite of its brilliant and intense ordering, seems so close to life that I wonder why its absurdity has not, for its readers, completely, finally and absolutely extirpated even the remotest possibility of being an actor in such a scene at any time whatever, let alone every day. But it is all too lamentably obvious that it has not. So in what sense, precisely, does literature 'teach' us? That it does seems clear. But how?

3 Deception

If we take Emma and Mr Knightley, at their best, as constituting some kind of norm of excellence (or elegance – see the Conclusion) then it is obvious that much of the novel consists of deviations from this by most of the characters and most of all by Emma herself. The clearest of these are the various kinds of deception, conscious and unconscious, with which the reader is entertained. *Emma* is quite often called a 'detective novel' – one of the first, etc., etc. Such a description is the one flaw in Ronald Blythe's otherwise excellent introduction to the Penguin edition. But if taken seriously this is, surely, very misleading: (a) because there is no crime, no detective and only one intrigue which the reader does not immediately understand; (b) because it would place the Frank Churchill/ Jane Fairfax relationship as the major source of interest, which it obviously and deliberately is not; and (c) because it indicates, possibly unfairly, a sort of light and temporary excitement (of the crossword puzzle kind) which the novel is, among other things, bound to disappoint – thus resembling the sale of Nietzsche's *The Gay Science* in a plain wrapper a few years ago. Nevertheless one can see why the description 'detective novel' might be offered in a fit of cleverness. For the condition of ignorance about oneself and others *is* pervasive – as pervasive as it is in life and in *Northanger Abbey, Sense and Sensibility, Pride and Prejudice, Mansfield Park, Persuasion, Sanditon* and other novels. An obvious example is the initial triangle between Emma, Harriet and Mr Elton. Here everything is clear to the reader and nothing to the characters – a state of affairs which makes for almost continuous comedy. Emma's fantasies about the sweet and stupid Harriet are so strong that they even turn the misfortune of bastardy into a promise of noble birth. They are usually attributed to a mixture of snobbery and the wanton and patronizing desire to control people in Emma's hobby of 'match-making'. But, while these elements are certainly present, a careful reading will probably find their source in her intellectual solitude ('Highbury ... afforded her no equals'). A powerful romantic imagination – of which Jane Austen is characteristically wary – creates a Harriet that only occasionally coincides with the real girl. Actually Emma is under no serious illusions about her friend and the kind of advantages she offers:

... a Harriet Smith ... one whom one could summon at any time to a walk, would be a valuable addition to her privileges ... Harriet certainly was not clever, but she had a sweet, docile, grateful disposition; was totally free from conceit; and only desiring to be guided by any one she looked up to. (Chapter 4)

But her protégée must have a gentleman for a husband. Mr Elton – about whom she is almost equally patronizing to herself – will fit the bill; and therefore they must both carry out Emma's plan. The episode of Harriet's portrait in Chapter 6 is typical. Emma suggests it. Mr Elton, here created beautifully by his speech, gushes out his approval:

'Let me entreat you ... it would indeed be a delight! Let me entreat you, Miss Woodhouse, to exercise so charming a talent in favour of your friend. I know what your drawings are. How could you suppose me ignorant? Is not this room rich in specimens of your landscapes and flowers; and has not Mrs Weston some inimitable figure-pieces in her drawing-room, at Randalls?'

And Emma has made herself blind to his rather blatant intentions:

Yes, good man! – thought Emma – but what has all that to do with taking likenesses? You know nothing of drawing. Don't pretend to be in raptures about mine. Keep your raptures for Harriet's face.

The portrait completed, the responses of its critics echo and reinforce what we know of their personalities. Mrs Weston is gently but minutely critical; Mr Knightley direct – 'You have made her too tall, Emma'; Mr Woodhouse indulgent and benign, but worried about the dangers to the health of a person depicted as sitting outdoors; and Mr Elton 'in continual raptures' – about the artist, although he naturally has to seem to praise the sitter. Only poor Harriet, tellingly, has nothing to say. The effect is not mechanical, but vivacious. But when Emma makes Harriet refuse Robert Martin the comedy becomes graver and its negative aspect appears. Here she stoops to a slightly unpleasant, though still funny, hypocrisy. For (in Chapter 7) she is somewhat ruffled by reading Martin's sensible letter when it is offered by the eager and undecided Harriet. Yet she is quite unshaken and resorts to a deliberate misunderstanding of her friend's request for advice. She responds with an oppressive certainty – notice the play on the meanings of 'looking down':

> 'Well,' said the still waiting Harriet; 'well – and – and what shall I do?'
> 'What shall you do! In what respect? Do you mean with a regard to this letter?'
> 'Yes.'
> 'But what are you in doubt of? You must answer it of course – and speedily.'
> 'Yes. But what shall I say? Dear Miss Woodhouse, do advise me.'
> 'Oh, no, no! the letter had much better be all your own. You will express yourself very properly, I am sure ...'
> 'You think I ought to refuse him then,' said Harriet, looking down.
> 'Ought to refuse him! My dear Harriet, what do you mean? Are you in any doubt as to that?'

This is almost cruel. It is continued, with *brio*, in Emma's sustained pretence of impartiality:

> 'Miss Woodhouse, as you will not give me your opinion, I must do as well as I can by myself; and I have now quite determined, and really almost made up my mind – to refuse Mr Martin. Do you think I am right?'
> 'Perfectly, perfectly right, my dearest Harriet; you are doing just what you ought. While you were in suspense I kept my feelings to myself, but now that you are so completely decided I have no hesitation in approving.'

Hypocrite. Here Emma brings all the masterful intelligence which works so well in enforcing good sense to bear on a perverse end. Deceived by her own creation of a ladylike Harriet, she deceives Harriet.

However, deception in this early part of the novel is by no means all deliberate. It is rife. And much of it is the result of a kind of indolence which Jane Austen describes (in a famous passage) with delighted acerbity:

> Her views of improving her little friend's mind, by a great deal of useful reading and conversation, had never yet led to more than a first few chapters, and the

intention of going on to-morrow. It was much easier to chat than to study; much pleasanter to let her imagination range and work at Harriet's fortune, than to be labouring to enlarge her comprehension or exercise it on sober facts; and the only literary pursuit which engaged Harriet at present, the only mental provision she was making for the evening of her life, was the collecting and transcribing all the riddles of every sort that she could meet with, into a thin quarto of hot-pressed paper, made up by her friend, and ornamented with cyphers and trophies.

In this age of literature, such collections on a very grand scale are not uncommon.

The last sentence is an example of the element in Jane Austen's prose which is often appropriately called 'Johnsonian'. And the passage is an introduction to the hilarious episode of the charades in which Emma's sense is yet again defeated by her preoccupation. '"Thy ready wit the word will soon supply." Humph – Harriet's ready wit! All the better. A man must be very much in love indeed to describe her so. Ah! Mr Knightley, I wish you had the benefit of this . . .' We are quite pleased for her that he has not the benefit of her thoughts.

One of the many functions of deception or misunderstanding at this stage is to provide the context for important statements of meaning. I shall single out two. We have already seen that over Harriet Emma deceives herself in an almost deliberate way – pursuing her fancy while at the same time being quite clear as to the limitations of her protégée. We are soon made aware of a deeper blindness of which she is typically and comically proud. When (in Chapter 10) Harriet raises the question of marriage for her superior friend we are reminded of the 'danger . . . at present so unperceived' mentioned on the first page of the book. Emma lucidly and airily expounds her views of herself and her future:

'I have none of the usual inducements of women to marry. Were I to fall in love, indeed, it would be a different thing! But I never have been in love; it is not my way, or my nature; and I do not think I ever shall. And, without love, I am sure I should be a fool to change such a situation as mine. Fortune I do not want; employment I do not want; consequence I do not want . . .'

Such clarity – yet such childish complacency. Harriet urges the horror of being an old maid like Miss Bates. But Emma, while disparaging Miss Bates ('so silly – so satisfied – so smiling – so prosing – so undistinguishing and unfastidious'), is sure, with an unsentimental realism that might elsewhere convince us, that 'it is poverty only which makes celibacy contemptible to a generous public'. And then follows a crucial speech – about self-knowledge:

'If I know myself, Harriet, mine is an active, busy mind, with a great many independent resources; and I do not perceive why I should be more in want of employment at forty or fifty than one-and-twenty. Woman's usual occupations of eye and hand and mind will be as open to me then, as they are now; or with no important variation. If I draw less, I shall read more; if I give up music, I shall take to carpet-work. And as for objects of interest, objects for the affections, which is in truth the great point of inferiority, the want of which is really the great evil to be avoided in *not* marrying, I shall be very well off, with all the children of a sister I love so much, to care about. There will be enough of them, in all probability, to supply every sort of sensation that declining life can need. There will be enough for every hope and fear; and though my attachment to none can equal that of a parent, it suits my ideas of comfort better than what is warmer and blinder. My nephews and nieces! – I shall often have a niece with me.'

This could almost be a pastiche of the routine view of Jane Austen as a clever spinster. And its inadequacy is rendered by her in a particularly trenchant way. 'If I know myself ...' provokes the reader by its complacency. The subsequent ordered efficiency of Emma's thought is a perfect vehicle for the display of her emotional vacuity. Even in the ordering of recreations she blithely gives an equal value to music and carpet-work. And then, of course, she sees nephews and nieces as an emotional convenience – a 'comfort' to be used when she pleases. Little Henry in fact has a superb comic role later in the novel (Chapter 26) when used as a screen between Emma and her knowledge of her feelings for Mr Knightley. In a way the listing of occupations and comforts is even slightly pathetic. In spite of the confidence of tone we may be again reminded of the paucity of diversion, the limitations of fruitful activity in Highbury, and even, for women at least, of the actual impossibility of doing much at all to please oneself – except through the risky means of matrimony. One of the uses of Harriet for Emma is that with such a companion it is possible for a girl to go for a walk. Readers of that book will remember how in *Pride and Prejudice* Elizabeth causes a tiny and unladylike sensation by walking alone; and readers of this one will see significance in Jane Fairfax's resolute refusals of company. Even the despised Miss Bates probably makes (chaotic) lists of her comforts. For the moment Emma is proud. It is possible that she is also defiant. But the most remarkable phrase of all is 'warmer and blinder'. This is not the language we normally associate with Jane Austen. In context it suggests the more intimate aspects – physical and mental – of motherhood. And it perhaps suggests an uncomfortably keen insight on Emma's part into that whole area of life – the area of the instinctual – which her callow rationality is at pains to reject. If we took a flight into the generalities of literary history we might be tempted to remark that it is typical of the transition between the established order of 'Reason', etc., and the contemporary ('Romantic') push towards exploration of other areas of the psyche – but perhaps that is to speculate too portentously.

The whole passage, then, is an important demonstration of the way in which Emma is young in other than the fortunate and lively sense. The novel is, of course, as are very many novels, concerned with the growing up of the central characters. We now have full information about one serious area where Emma certainly needs education by experience. She gets it subsequently. But immediately Jane Austen goes on to reinforce this particular episode in a way with which we are familiar. She redresses the balance of feelings by an explicit statement of some of the virtues of the repellent person to whom we have been listening:

Emma was very compassionate; and the distresses of the poor were as sure of relief from her personal attention and kindness, her counsel and her patience, as from her purse. She understood their ways, could allow for their ignorance and their temptations, had no romantic expectations of extraordinary virtue from those, for whom education had done so little; entered into their troubles with ready sympathy, and always gave her assistance with as much intelligence as good-will.

She is reinstated in the reader's affection, or, at least, approval. She is emphatically not the kind of lady charity visitor to whom Dickens's bricklayer in *Bleak House* (1852–3) so magnificently replies:

'An't my place dirty? Yes, it is dirty – it's nat'rally dirty, and it's nat'rally onwholesome; and we've had five dirty and onwholesome children, as is all dead infants, and so much the better for them, and us besides. Have I read the little book wot you left? No, I an't read the little book wot you left ... It's a book fit for a babby and I'm not a babby. If you was to leave me a doll, I shouldn't nuss it. How have I been conducting of myself? Why, I've been drunk for three days; and I'd a been drunk four, if I'd a had the money. Don't I never mean to go to church? No, I don't never mean for to go to church. I shouldn't be expected there, if I did; the beadle's too gen-teel for me. And how did my wife get that black eye? Why I giv'it her; and if she says I didn't, she's a Lie!'

The second important sequence about deception at this stage in the novel is that dramatizing the collapse of Emma's fantasy about Harriet and Mr Elton, brought to its inevitable climax in his proposal to her after the Westons' dinner party. This produces a pleasurable embarrassment in the reader, but is an unforeseen and salutary humiliation for the heroine. We should note that although we are in the position of being able to predict what will happen, Emma heroically persists in her delusion to the very furthest point possible. Her 'hand seized – her attention demanded, and Mr Elton actually making violent love to her', she still thinks of him as 'Mr Elton, the lover of Harriet' – though not for long, of course. She is at this moment so obtuse (it is a few minutes after her decisive action with Mr Knightley in ending the dinner party) that we even feel some sympathy for the glutinous Elton; although he begins to resemble his fellow cleric, the portentous clown Mr Collins in *Pride and Prejudice* in his ill-bred inability to take no for an answer ('Charming Miss Woodhouse! Allow me to interpret this interesting silence. It confesses that you have long understood me'), he has at least some justification in having been genuinely deceived.

Emma is still a heroine, however. Her rigorous examination of herself and all the circumstances in the ensuing Chapter 16 is quite free from self-pity and, even more interestingly, *not* the grovelling collapse we might expect from a more commonplace person. The reader may sense an invitation to take her derogatory summary of her suitor as an unwitting summary of herself:

> Mr Elton was proving himself, in many respects, the very reverse of what she had meant and believed him; proud, assuming, conceited; very full of his own claims, and little concerned about the feelings of others.

The 'she had meant ... him' is charming. The challenge is effective. But most of the rest of her interior monologue (let alone the rest of the action) tends against so bluntly efficient and ironical a device. She has been humiliated; but her first thought is for Harriet – 'compared with the evil to Harriet, all was light'. And she quickly acknowledges the standards from which she has strayed. 'To Mr John Knightley she was indebted for her first idea on the subject' and as for his brother, she 'blushed to think how much truer a knowledge of ... character had been ... shewn than any she had reached herself. It was dreadfully mortifying ...' Actually Mr Knightley has been nothing like so dismissive of Mr Elton as she now believes him to have been. But she is very much concerned with the feelings of others.

Her thoughts are, typically, a see-saw of honesty and delusion. The honesty is real. So much so that it may not appeal to the modern reader:

> Sighs and fine words had been given in abundance; but she could hardly devise any set of expressions, or fancy any tone of voice, less allied with real love. She need not trouble herself to pity him. He only wanted to aggrandize and enrich himself; and if Miss Woodhouse of Hartfield, the heiress of thirty thousand pounds, were not quite so easily obtained as he had fancied, he would soon try for Miss Somebody else with twenty, or with ten.

This is harsh, but also true. Emma may not yet know what real love sounds like, but the reader has heard for himself what it does not. And Mr Elton soon secures 'so many thousands as would always be called ten' with his Augusta. Equally acute is:

Perhaps it was not fair to expect him to feel how very much he was her inferior in talent, and all the elegancies of mind. The very want of such equality might prevent his perception of it ...

Again a hard piece of charity, involving a subtle perception. And we cannot even deny the justness of her social judgement – 'in fortune and consequence she was greatly his superior ... the Eltons were nobody'. But however accurate all this may be it would hardly be endearing if she did turn the same precise light onto herself. 'Emma was obliged in common honestly to stop and admit that her own behaviour to him had been so complaisant and obliging' as to justify him. Crucially:

The first error and the worst lay at her door. It was foolish, it was wrong, to take so active a part in bringing any two people together. It was adventuring too far, assuming too much, making light of what ought to be serious, a trick of what ought to be simple.

Such gravity is appropriate. But where are we? Surely not a third of the way through a great comic novel? It is even more appropriate that the old Adam in Emma, as it were, suddenly reappears. 'Concerned and ashamed, and resolved' to do no more match-making as she is, she casually reflects that she was nevertheless right to dash the hopes of 'young Martin' and to give Harriet 'the opportunity of pleasing some one worth having' – perhaps one William Coxe; but 'Oh! no, I could not endure William Coxe – a pert young lawyer.' Emma checks herself, but Emma is herself again. And this passage of serious introspection is promisingly rounded off with:

To youth and cheerfulness like Emma's, though under temporary gloom at night, the return of day will hardly fail to bring return of spirits.

Charming Miss Woodhouse indeed.

4 Intrigue

From deception emerges intrigue: a real 'plot' to further the Plot. Almost from the beginning the aristocratic Churchills have been looming off-stage. And Chapter 18 starts on a significant note: 'Mr Frank Churchill did not come.' Absence, or silence in company, is a well-known way of magnifying importance. The pipe-smoker with pregnant puffs and pauses seems to emphasize the profundity of his opinions. The late arrival often meets with as much respect as he does resentment. And this is even more the case in an ordered work of art where accident only apparently rules. Mr Knightley's utterances are the weightier because of their relative rarity. And the long build-up to Frank Churchill's entrance deliberately causes speculation and excitement among both characters and readers. Will he come? When will he come? What will he be like? Jane Austen is playing very humorously with the artistic convention of preludes and fanfares before the entrance of the young male lead, the *jeune premier*, the tenor role to contrast with Mr Knightley's established baritone. Emma plays with the notion too – shortly before the claustrophic realities of Mr Elton's proposal in the carriage:

> Now, it so happened that in spite of Emma's resolution of never marrying, there was something in the name, in the idea of Mr Frank Churchill, which always interested her. She had frequently thought ... that if she *were* to marry, he was the very person to suit her in age, character and condition ... she had a great curiosity to see him, a decided intention of finding him pleasant, of being liked by him to a certain degree, and a sort of pleasure in the idea of their being coupled in their friends' imaginations.
>
> With such sensations, Mr Elton's civilities were dreadfully ill-timed ...
>
> (Chapter 14)

But still he does not come to visit his new mother-in-law, and Chapter 18 provides even more interesting premonitions – this time in the form of Mr Knightley's severities about the delay. Note that Emma, in conducting the defence, 'perceived that she was taking the other side of the question from her real opinion'. More importantly, the chapter is really about Mr Knightley and tells little about Frank that we do not already know; Mr Knightley is consciously decisive, but unconsciously self-revelatory.

> 'If Frank Churchill had wanted to see his father, he would have contrived it between September and January. A man at his age – what is he? three or four-and-twenty – cannot be without the means of doing as much as that. It is impossible.'

Mr Knightley is 'about seven or eight-and-thirty', as we know. And for some reason he seems unable to leave the question alone. Emma objects that Frank is dependent on the Churchills – 'You do not know what it is to have tempers to manage.' But:

> 'It is not to be conceived in a man of three or four-and-twenty should not have liberty of mind or limb to that amount ... We hear of him for ever at some watering-place or other.'

Further, the poor young man can easily travel 'whenever he thinks it worth his while; whenever there is any temptation of pleasure'. Mr Knightley is right, as usual, but he seems to have lost his usual tolerance and humour. What is Frank to him, that he should be so fiercely adamant?

> 'There is one thing, Emma, which a man can always do, if he chuses, and that is, his duty; not by manoeuvring and finessing, but by vigour and resolution. It is Frank Churchill's duty to pay this attention to his father.'

45

And he composes a declaration of independence which Frank might use on Mrs Churchill. Emma laughs at him, and lets slip an important compliment: 'Nobody but you, Mr Knightley, would imagine it possible.' But there is no getting past the point:

'Respect for right conduct is felt by every body. If he would act in this sort of manner, on principle, consistently, regularly, their little minds would bend to his.'

Nor will Emma's affectionate badinage – 'You are very fond of bending little minds' – deflect him. In the end it comes down to the admirable:

'No, Emma, your amiable young man can be amiable only in French – not in English. He may be very "aimable", have very good manners, and be very agreeable; but he can have no English delicacy towards the feelings of other people; nothing really amiable about him.'

At last the conversation becomes explicitly what it has really been all along: personal. Emma objects that Mr Knightley seems determined to think ill of Frank, and this hits the nerve:

'Me! – not at all,' replied Mr Knightley, rather displeased; 'I do not want to think ill of him. I should be as ready to acknowledge his merits as any other man ...'

But on Emma's stressing Frank's probable importance as a social acquisition (a real point, as we have seen), he becomes positively indignant:

'What! At three-and-twenty to be the king of his company – the great man ... My dear Emma, your own good sense could not endure such a puppy when it came to the point.'

Emma persists in trying to make peace by saying that they are both prejudiced on the subject. But this only makes things worse. 'Prejudiced! I am not prejudiced.'

'He is a person I never think of from one month's end to another,' said Mr Knightley, with a degree of vexation, which made Emma immediately talk of something else, though she could not comprehend why he should be so angry.

No doubt *we* can, by now. The repeated, and funny, references to Frank's youth do the trick; they combine with the unwarranted agitation to make Mr Knightley 'unjust to the merit of another' and so join Emma, for once, in deviation from the norm of good sense and good feeling. But still Frank Churchill does not come.

Instead Jane Fairfax – that living reproach to Emma in beauty and elegance – is introduced. Her one fault to an Emma determined to do her justice lies in her unforthcomingness about Frank, her reserve. She has met him but will not tell. '"Was he handsome?" – "She believed he was reckoned to be a very fine young man." "Was he agreeable?" – "He was generally thought so." "Did he appear a sensible young man; a young man of information?"' – In short, since we know he is rich, is he handsome and clever too? – '"She believed every body found his manners pleasing."' (Chapter 20.) We may well be nearly as irritated by this bland reliance on the general as is Emma who 'could not forgive her', for the moment anyway. But Mr Knightley is pleased with her arrival because he 'had been used to think [Emma] unjust to Jane, and had now great pleasure in marking an improvement'. The upshot of this is that we learn quite a lot about Jane; more of Emma's quickness and warmth; more about whom Mr Knightley is mainly interested in – and again nothing about Frank. Surely it is time for the entrance?

But no. First Miss Bates garbles out the sensational news, in this community, of Mr Elton's engagement, thus allowing Jane Austen a famous 'Johnsonian' remark relating to that community:

> Human nature is so well disposed towards those who are in interesting situations, that a young person, who either marries or dies, is sure of being kindly spoken of. (Chapter 22)

The sting of this lies in its accuracy: it is either acid or teasing, depending upon how you take it. Next, or, rather, in counterpoint, the interest of Harriet in Robert Martin is revived. Both are wreathed in breathless inconsequence. Emma is bored and exasperated – 'her mind was quite sick of Mr Elton and the Martins' – and possibly her creator is too, to judge from the sharpness of her tone. So, at last, Frank is coming. He now arrives *early* – a beautiful effect of bathos. And he is exactly, in appearance, speech and action, what he is expected to be: a surprise in offering no surprises.

The concealed intrigue centred on Frank and Jane Fairfax now becomes the source from which most of the misunderstandings about who is to marry whom (that is, most of the surface interest of the novel) derive. It is itself full of clues and jokes: the haircut, the pianoforté, Emma's tremendous and reprehensible speculations about the Dixons, the alphabet game with its 'blunder', Jane's behaviour at Donwell, and very many lesser and more subtle indications. There is even an incident, at the beginning of Chapter 44, when Emma visits Jane and Jane will not be seen, where we are led to expect a mystery only to find immediately that there is none. Presumably all this is where the 'detective story' argument finds its less than interesting justification. I cannot remember at what point on first reading I tumbled on the truth. Readers will obviously differ. But certainly a knowledge, or even a strong suspicion, of the secret engagement enhances our pleasure, not least in noting Frank's cheerful but by no means entirely pleasant duplicities. Like Emma at her worst he very much enjoys playing games with people, including Emma herself. Unlike Emma he does not tell the truth. When he goes too far, he could wound deeply. Since most of the novel is seen from Emma's point of view we are not encouraged or even allowed (this is a useful 'technical' point) to take a painful stance. But what if she had fallen in love with him? What about poor Harriet, even? As it is, Jane Fairfax really suffers. Mr Knightley is right in his unfair prediction, even if he does not deserve to be: Frank has 'no English delicacy towards the feelings of other people'. Which, of course, is very far from making him a villain on the model of, say, Richardson's Lovelace in *Clarissa*. Lovelace is a more interesting man, but of a type, deliberately and brilliantly evil yet vulnerable because of his sensitivity, in which Jane Austen does not deal.

In any case it seems likely that even the least alert reader should be pretty well in the know by the time of the spectacle mending, piano-leg propping episode in Chapter 28 – that is, about fifty pages after Frank's entrance. And nobody except Emma could be in much doubt when, at his first departure and in genuine if temporary contrition, he only just fails to come clean with her. But the great focal point of this sequence, as of so much else in the book, is the outing to Box Hill in Chapter 43. There it is evident once again that the central subject is Emma and her relationship to Mr Knightley. It is also the climax of her deviation from the norm they together represent.

This excursion, like the family dinner in Chapter 12, is supposed to be an occasion for pleasure. Like that, too, it is dominated by pettiness, unease, and tempers barely kept. But this time the restraints of good sense fail, and Emma, instead of being a politely active force for harmony, is the worst offender. She is closely seconded in silliness by Frank, for whom the episode is also a watershed.

Jane Austen's weather is never accidental. The snow at the Westons' was associated with the Elton débâcle: now the summer produces its own bad side. 'They had a very fine day for Box Hill; and all the ... outward circumstances ... were in favour of a pleasant party.' But the heat, entirely realistically, produces frayed tempers and excess. It was bad enough at the strawberry-picking at Donwell in the previous chapter (see Mrs Elton's extremely funny disconnected monologue on fruit and heat), but as Emma says, 'It is hotter today.' The 'languour ... want of spirits ... want of union, which could not be got over' result in an irritation and boredom which must be familiar to every reader. They naturally in turn produce in Emma and Frank a frustrated top-of-the-head gaiety and frivolity, brilliantly described – or, rather, shown in speech. On such occasions it is obligatory to enjoy oneself and be amusing:

'Ladies and gentlemen, I am ordered by Miss Woodhouse (who, wherever she is, presides,) to say, that she desires to know what you are all thinking of.'

A terrible demand, in response to which Mr Knightley's 'Is Miss Woodhouse sure that you would like to hear what we are all thinking of?' strikes one as very moderate. Emma herself is embarrassed by Frank's remorseless playfulness and flirtation:

Not that Emma was gay and thoughtless from any real felicity; it was rather because she felt less happy than she had expected. She laughed because she was disappointed . . .

Nevertheless – or rather therefore – the prevailing mood causes her to commit one of those shaming clever indiscretions, the memory of which can haunt its author for years. To the rather unexpected clarity and self-knowledge of Miss Bates about dullness, she responds with something often thought but which should never have been expressed:

'Oh! very well,' exclaimed Miss Bates, 'then I need not be uneasy. "Three things very dull indeed." That will just do for me, you know. I shall be sure to say three dull things as soon as ever I open my mouth, shan't I? – (looking round with the most good-humoured dependence on every body's assent) – Do not you all think I shall?'

Emma could not resist.

'Ah! ma'am, but there may be a difficulty. Pardon me – but you will be limited as to number – only three at once.'

Miss Bates, deceived by the mock ceremony of her manner, did not immediately catch her meaning; but, when it burst upon her, it could not anger, though a slight blush showed that it could pain her.

'Ah! – well – to be sure. Yes, I see what she means . . .'

It is possible that Emma, miffed by Mr Knightley's liking for Jane, feels unusually impatient with the Bates household in general. But Frank, of course, is right. Whatever Mrs Elton's obtuse claims, in Highbury Emma 'wherever she is, presides'. The easy witticism is a serious breakdown in 'delicacy towards the feelings of other people'. And, in Jane Austen's scheme at any rate, it is essential that people enjoying superiority earn it by their behaviour if they are to be admired. (I shall be looking at the exact reverse in Sir Walter Elliot in *Persuasion*.) Note that in this novel Mr Woodhouse's position is only tolerable because of his humility, and Mr Knightley's because of his character. So a trivial insult to one who is an inferior in every sense is nearly unforgivable. It is true that Mrs Elton's rebuke is so awful as to remind us of what Emma, fortunately, is not:

'I am not one of those who have witty things at every body's service. I do not pretend to be a wit. I have a great deal of vivacity in my own way, but I really must be allowed to judge when to speak and when to hold my tongue. Pass us, if you please, Mr Churchill. Pass Mr E., Knightley, Jane, and myself. We have nothing clever to say – not one of us.'

But the atmosphere remains. Frank airily and uneasily goes on to hurt Jane Fairfax by talking at random and is so disturbed by the implications of her grave, cloaked rebuke that his 'spirits now rose to a pitch almost unpleasant'. At last the festivities end and Emma rightly feels that 'Such another scheme, composed of so many ill-assorted people, she hoped never to be betrayed into again.' But of course she cannot hope to escape present consequences. Mr Knightley's rebuke is as just as it is inevitable. It clearly costs him effort and pain to talk so severely – and at such unaccustomed length. It is a tribute to Emma's real qualities, her honest sensitivity, that he has an even greater effect than he can have desired. After her lame efforts at defence she becomes mute, and things are made worse by silence:

> He had misinterpreted the feelings which had kept her face averted, and her tongue motionless. They were combined only of anger against herself, mortification, and deep concern ... He had turned away, and the horses were in motion. She continued to look back, but in vain ... She was vexed beyond what could have been expressed – almost beyond what she could conceal. Never had she felt so agitated, mortified, grieved, at any circumstance in her life. She was most forcibly struck. The truth of his representation there was no denying. She felt it at her heart. How could she have been so brutal, so cruel to Miss Bates! – How could she have exposed herself to such ill opinion in any one she valued! And to suffer him to leave her without saying one word of gratitude, of concurrence, of common kindness!
>
> Time did not compose her ...

This is much worse than the aftermath of Mr Elton's proposal. The peculiar chagrin Emma feels is, as so often in Jane Austen and in reality, compounded by the randomness of communication imposed by social relations. Time and opportunity to meet and explain are needed. But they cannot easily be commanded by any individual. When can Emma present a truer impression? A chance missed may be missed for ever, and the whole direction of a life determined in a casual moment or by a conventional inhibition. Brutus remarks of much greater doings:

> There is a tide in the affairs of men,
> Which, taken at the flood, leads on to fortune;
> Omitted, all the voyage of their life
> Is bound in shallows and in miseries.
>
> (*Julius Caesar*, IV. 3)

But in *Emma* there is a second chance which, though precarious, leads on to happier things.

*

The climax of the 'intrigue' then evolves into the climax of the whole book. The effects are not, of course, confined to Emma and Frank. The behaviour of the latter in particular allows everyone so inclined to modify and deepen their favourite self-deception. Mr Knightley, as we have seen, is bound to be confirmed in his painful jealousy of the younger man – an illusion shared quite naturally by all who have ordinary expectations of the 'boy meets girl' (or rather 'they are made for each other') kind. The Westons, Mr and Mrs John Knightley, the Bateses, the Eltons – even, probably, William Coxe – cannot be blamed for expecting a conclusion so apparently foregone. Harriet is important in developing feelings, like Frankenstein's monster, which quite outstrip the predictions and wishes of their creator – and this takes place and is blindly encouraged by the latter because of the fine misunderstanding between them bred by Frank's presence and the role he plays. Finally, poor Jane Fairfax is bound to be misunderstood by everyone because of her half-unwilling complicity. Her relations with Emma become more and more strained; Mrs Elton is allowed to push her into a false situation as client – and almost a real 'situation'; Frank teases her even in his good nature; her relations with the Campbells and the Dixons are subject to gross misrepresentation, especially by the exuberant Emma; Miss Bates grieves – and so on. But since the details of this miasma are plain enough, exasperating enough, and funny enough to any reader it would be futile to detail them further here. They are all parts of the very complex whole which revolves around the main theme, to which I now turn.

5 Marriage and Sexuality

It is often said – perhaps *ad nauseam* – that *Emma* is a novel 'about' marriage. But the extent and implications of this statement are not so often realized. The main theme plays around Emma herself, of course. But consider how many marriages besides her own the novel involves. It opens with that of Miss Taylor to Mr Weston – and among the results of this are Emma's involvement with Harriet and thus with Mr Elton, and the special interest aroused by Frank Churchill. An indirect spin-off of Mr Elton's rejection is the ghastly descent of his alternative bride, a *pis aller* who threatens to dominate, not without some success, the middle portion of the book. Mrs Elton proves an adroit exploiter of her privileged position as a newly married person (a privilege, incidentally, which seems to have disappeared from English society). And at the end there are three further marriages – the appropriate and fitting products of the complex interweavings of the action.

It is often objected of this and comparable novels (including all of Jane

Austen's) that the happy ending so triumphantly arrived at stops disappointingly at the church door. The book is not so much about marriage as about the necessary preparations and preconditions for it; about courtship, in fact. This is a good point but not, if we reflect, an entirely accurate one. For there are various studies of marriage in progress, so to speak, in all the subsidiary parts. There is a new marriage of middle-aged people (the Westons) which has its own particular tone of accommodating happiness. There is a new marriage of young people (the Eltons) which may represent a harmony of minds but which shows the man's coarser tendencies flowering under the influence of his wife – his behaviour to Harriet at the Ball, for instance, is far too ungentlemanly, far too mean, for the harmless careerist to whom we are first introduced. And there is an established marriage of the young middle-aged (the John Knightleys) which very amusingly shows the mutual adaptation and happiness of the conventionally grumpy and businesslike yet home-loving man and the equally conventional fussy and domestic budding matron – a union which overflows with children (there are no others, save perhaps Emma, in the novel), including Little Henry. All these are the subject of drama and comment throughout. And, apart from the interest which they themselves offer, their main function, together with the other two unions at the end, is to provide an essential set of comparisons and contrasts for our judgement of the most important marriage of all: that between Emma and George Knightley. Through them we see what that is, and what, fortunately, it is not.

Who can say, then, that marriage is not the subject? Even Miss Bates contributes, in her way, to it. And, in fact, a contemplation of the subject reveals the one problem in the book which may be considered a flaw. We are bound to speculate as to how the late Mrs Woodhouse, evidently a woman of considerable sense if we take into account the probabilities of heredity at all, could possibly have married and continued to be married to Mr Woodhouse, an unrelievedly stupid man, and importantly, 'a valetudinarian all his life, without activity of mind and body'? Compare the care with which in *Persuasion* Anne Elliot's mother is recalled as 'an excellent woman, sensible, and amiable; whose judgement and conduct, if they might be pardoned the youthful infatuation which made her Lady Elliot, had never required indulgence afterwards', and after whom her daughter so obviously takes. Or compare, for that matter, the suffering endured and the damage done to Mr Bennet in *Pride and Prejudice* because of a similar and disastrous capitulation to brainless beauty. There are other examples in Jane Austen, too numerous to mention. On the other hand this *is* speculation only and I doubt if many readers are deterred by it long, if at all.

*

A more serious objection concerns sex. Courtship and marriage undoubtedly involve physical attraction – or, at least, we think (unlike many other cultures) that they *should*. It is possible that many contemporary unions are based on it alone, and are therefore regretted when the bloom is off the rose and if no other bonds save habit and obligation are, by serendipity, found. I have the idea that quite a number of readers are disappointed by their impression that, while Jane Austen is wonderfully acute in sifting, evaluating, and dramatizing all the other facts of mind, spirit, morals, taste and social compatibility that should make a marriage successful or otherwise, she is primly weak on all the interesting and glittering features of physical fascination. After all she was a spinster and probably did not know ..., etc. And to complicate the problem, it is certainly a peculiar piece of history that the efflorescence of the great realistic literary form, the novel, should have coincided so awkwardly with that period when, in England at least, everyone suddenly became prudish and repressed. Every schoolchild knows that the Victorians covered even the legs of pianos. They probably now know in the same manner that this often resulted in the most scandalous double lives, a seething hypocrisy. And for this purpose Jane Austen may as well have been a Victorian – see, for example, the unfortunate passage quoted from D. H. Lawrence.

The first thing to notice is that direct presentation of sex in art is actually rather boring. A kiss *is* just a kiss except to the lovers – and this applies *a fortiori* to related activities. Henry James made the point that there is (normally) very little variation beyond the bedroom door. Even Lawrence himself, I feel, nobly failed in his full frontal attack on the question in *Lady Chatterley's Lover*. And who has not been bored, when they are not embarrassed, by the results of the conviction of *derrière garde* film or television producers that a double bed, a sheet, and two fine torsos guarantee entertainment?

But this does not solve the problem. Sexual attraction does, indeed, matter. Consider the following from *The Golden Bowl* by Henry James:

He saw again that her thick hair was, vulgarly speaking, brown, but that there was a shade of tawny autumn leaf in it, for 'appreciation' – a colour indescribable and of which he had known no other case, something that gave her at moments the sylvan head of a huntress. He saw the sleeves of her jacket drawn to her wrists, but he again made out the free arms within them to be of the completely rounded, the polished slimness that Florentine sculptors, in the great time, had loved, and of which the apparent firmness is expressed in their old silver and old bronze. He knew her narrow hands, he knew her long fingers and the shape and colour of her finger-nails, he knew her special beauty of movement and line when she turned her back, and the perfect working of all her main attachments, that of some wonderful finished instrument, something intently made for exhibition, for a prize. He knew above all the extraordinary fineness of her flexible waist, the stem of an expanded flower which gave her a likeness also to some long, loose silk purse, well filled with gold pieces, but having been passed, empty, through a finger ring that held it together.   (Book 1, Chapter 3)

The multiple emphases on money and artifice here are important to the whole novel: but the local effect is very sensual indeed. Especially the finger-nails. Much more so than direct descriptions of sexy young women (or men) usually are. Jane Austen, similarly oblique, is very different. But she too works in this field by association rather than by a plain listing of points. Is Emma attractive physically? Is Mr Knightley a handsome man? We have to look quite hard to find explicit answers to such questions, and then we tend to find that the appearance of the lesser characters is more stressed than that of the principals. Harriet's 'soft blue eyes', etc., are what she has to offer, and Frank is obviously good looking. Of Mr Knightley we learn very little, and that gradually. Emma herself has to wait until a discussion of her in Chapter 5. 'Can you imagine any thing nearer perfect beauty than Emma altogether ... ?' says Mrs Weston. Mr Knightley in his role as a 'partial old friend' agrees. Mrs Weston insists:

'Such an eye! – the true hazel eye – and so brilliant! regular features, open countenance, with a complexion! oh! what a bloom of full health, and such a pretty height and size; such a firm and upright figure. There is health, not merely in her bloom, but in her air, her head, her glance ... She is loveliness itself. Mr Knightley, is not she?'
'I have no fault to find with her person,' he replied. 'I think her all you describe. I love to look at her; and I will add this praise, that I do not think her personally vain.'

This is satisfying enough. Nevertheless the description is not very particular, and seems almost as much about Emma's fine spirit as about her appearance – or, rather, the one is expressed in the other.

Then why is that we do end up with a strong view about how these people look, of their living presence? That we do is indicated by the fervour with which readers praise or denounce the casting in adaptations of novels for the screen or stage (I remember not being able to prove that a Mr Knightley on television did not look the part at all; and still feel that I was right). It is something of a mystery. It is equally mysterious that the most apparently glamorous couple, Frank and Jane, are comparatively lacking in physical presence. Both are explicitly praised – but the impression, deliberately, is relatively pale, like Jane's complexion. This goes with her reserve. And it of course suggests that any answer should be looked for in the behaviour of the characters – in which art again resembles life.

*

We thus return, obviously, to the central relationship between Mr Knightley and Emma. This not only provides the moral norm and the ultimate standard established in the book: it is also the chief love story. But it is in no obvious sense 'romantic'. Is it, except for a rather formal correctness, recognizably a story involving feelings and desires at all? Does not Emma marry an excellent older man, an uncle, rather than a proper hero? Compare the dashing Captain Wentworth with whom Kipling fancied Jane Austen in love – or, for that matter, the witty and glamorous Henry Tilney or the magnificent Mr Darcy. Are some readers not right in feeling a more or less explicit disappointment with the staid and thirty-eight-year-old Mr Knightley? I think that these problems had been foreseen by Jane Austen, and answered negatively and with force.

We learn from the very beginning that Mr Knightley has known and been close to Emma since she was a child. That his feelings are not simply avuncular is established by a series of hints like those just quoted from Chapter 5. But for a long time, possibly agreeing with the reader who thinks that youth should have youth, he remains resigned to the position of 'partial old friend' – and this in spite of his outburst against the idea of Frank Churchill. As for Emma, she of course is not going to marry anyway, and is perhaps too familiar with and a little too frightened of her affectionate but formidable corrector to entertain any conscious thoughts on the matter. Only towards the middle of the book, and in the context of the various misunderstandings and intrigues about love, do different feelings begin to emerge. And they emerge, satisfyingly, as unconscious or intuitive promptings. (It is interesting, by the way, to observe that part of the revolutionary force of Charlotte Brontë, who thought Jane Austen disablingly insipid, lay in her presentation of the love of young women for authoritative older men – in both *Jane Eyre* (1847) and *Villette* (1853).)

In Chapter 26 Mrs Weston, victim of the Frank/Jane deception, and intent on her own wishes for Frank and Emma, comes out with a bright idea:

'The more I think of it, the more probable it appears. In short, I have made a match between Mr Knightley and Jane Fairfax. See the consequence of keeping you company! – What do you say to it?'

The great match-maker herself has just described Mr Knightley as 'not a gallant man, but ... a very humane one' and she is therefore naturally surprised. But mere surprise would not account for her subsequent dismay and her catching at a ludicrous reason for her vehemence:

'Dear Mrs Weston, how could you think of such a thing? – Mr Knightley! – Mr Knightley must not marry! – You would not have little Henry cut out from

Donwell? – Oh! no, no, Henry must have Donwell. I cannot at all consent to Mr Knightley's marrying; I am sure it is not at all likely. I am amazed that you should think of such a thing.'

Against this, Mrs Weston reasons in vain:

'... I do not want to injure dear little Henry – but the idea has been given me by circumstances; and if Mr Knightley really wished to marry, you would not have him refrain on Henry's account, a boy of six years old, who knows nothing of the matter?'

'Yes, I would. I could not bear to have Henry supplanted. – Mr Knightley marry! – No, I have never had such an idea, and I cannot adopt it now ... Jane Fairfax mistress of the Abbey! – Oh! no, no; – every feeling revolts. For his own sake, I would not have him do so mad a thing.'

'Mad'? Why such violence on Emma's part? As Mrs Weston with unconscious slyness points out, there is only 'a little disparity of age' – and Emma and Jane are contemporaries. Emma's reaction resembles that of Mr Knightley to Frank. It differs from that in having no convincing conscious argument to back it up. It is delightful to the reader; and presumably not explicable to Emma. The splendid thing about the novel is that they are both instinctively correct about Frank and Jane while having no right to be.

Emma now begins, revealingly, to rationalize Mr Knightley's way of life in exactly the same manner as she has reasoned of her own. Little Henry is succeeded by a list:

'Why should he marry? – He is as happy as possible by himself; with his farm, and his sheep, and his library, and all the parish to manage; and he is extremely fond of his brother's children. He has no occasion to marry, either to fill up his time or his heart.'

This conversation gives us much else to ponder on. But it is certain that, from this point in the novel at the latest, we are witnessing the real convention – that Emma must marry Mr Knightley – in strenuous counterpoint with the specious one – that Emma should marry Frank. It is a foregone conclusion, however many times we have read the book (including the first); but it is always a tense drama. Moreover it is not all confined to large scenes or episodes, but is constantly alluded to in tiny details. For example, when in Chapter 34 handwriting is discussed and the main question seems to be whether Emma can bear to mention that of her 'suitor', Frank, Mr Knightley incidentally asserts that Isabella's hand is very similar to Emma's – '"Yes", said his brother hesitatingly, "there is a likeness. I know what you mean – but Emma's hand is the strongest."' It is not like him to hesitate in his opinions, but the fact that this and his remark could easily be passed over in reading is further indicative of both the density of Jane Austen's prose and of the control with which she picks out her themes in seemingly neutral contexts. In fact, no context is allowed to be neutral.

By this stage, too, the field has temporarily been cleared of contenders. Frank's somewhat tongue-tied departure in Chapter 30 has led to Emma's conviction that he must (after a fortnight) be in love with her. Her version of logic on these matters therefore demands that she be in love with him:

'I certainly must,' said she. 'This sensation of listlessness, weariness, stupidity, this disinclination to sit down and employ myself, this feeling of every thing's being dull and insipid about the house! – I must be in love; I should be the oddest creature in the world if I were not – for a few weeks at least.'

One perhaps knows the feeling. But boredom does not entertain Emma for long, and the patness of her quick recovery and the charming smugness of her reflection on it are entirely individual:

'I shall do very well again after a little while – and then, it will be a good thing over; for they say every body is in love once in their lives, and I shall have been let off easily.'

(Chapter 31)

It is the tone of 'If I know myself, Harriet . . .' all over again. In a manner equally characteristic of *him*, Mr Knightley soon disposes of the Fairfax question:

'No – till Cole alluded to my supposed attachment, it had never entered my head. I saw Jane Fairfax and conversed with her, with admiration and pleasure always – but with no thought beyond.'

(Chapter 33)

This is all clear enough, given its constant changeability. But what, the reader may ask, of sexual attraction? Of physical presence? This is partly implicit in the action and speech of the characters, as I have argued. But it is at the ball at the Crown – an occasion for physical consciousness and display, after all – that it appears almost explicitly. Again Emma's thoughts are the medium:

She was more disturbed by Mr Knightley's not dancing, than by any thing else. – There he was, among the standers-by, where he ought not to be; he ought to be dancing, – not classing himself with the husbands, and fathers, and whist-players, who were pretending to feel an interest in the dance till their rubbers were made up . . .

(Chapter 38)

Although used unobtrusively, the dance, especially of the ordered and formal nature envisaged here, is one of the great traditional modes and metaphors for courtship – or flirtation. The reader will remember from literature, perhaps from life, the great significance attached to choosing a partner, or being chosen, or being ignored or refused. No other social activity creates such sexual tension. A wallflower is almost synonomous with a spinster. Readers of *War and Peace* will remember Natasha's first ball. Indeed a first ball, or its equivalent, was, as it were, the first step into adult life: a kind of proclamation of nubility. Hence the safety net of equal numbers. Hence the vulgar savagery of Mr Elton's snub of Harriet a little later, the significance of Mr Knightley's intervention, and the unfortunate direction taken therefore by Harriet's thoughts. That a dance is usually thought of as an activity for the young is a matter of physical fitness, but not of the athletic kind. T. S. Eliot, writing in 1940, quotes the words of his ancestor Sir Thomas Elyot, writing in 1531:

> ... In that open field
> If you do not come too close, if you do not come too close,
> On a summer midnight, you can hear the music
> Of the weak pipe and the little drum
> And see them dancing round the bonfire
> The association of man and woman
> In daunsinge, signifying matrimonie –
> A dignified and commodious sacrament.
> Two and two, necessarye coniunction,
> Holding eche other by the hand or the arm
> Whiche betokeneth concorde ...

(East Coker)

Jane Austen in her entirely different way is drawing quite naturally, as she had done earlier in *Northanger Abbey*, on the same tradition. Mr Knightley 'ought' not join the dull older people, according to Emma's sudden recognition – 'so young as he looked!'. She continues:

He could not have appeared to greater advantage perhaps any where, than where he had placed himself. His tall, firm, upright figure, among the bulky forms and stooping shoulders of the elderly men, was such as Emma felt must draw every body's eyes; and, excepting her own partner, there was not one among the whole row of young men who could be compared with him. – He moved a few steps nearer, and those few steps were enough to prove in how gentlemanlike a manner, with what natural grace, he must have danced, would he but take the trouble. – Whenever she caught his eye, she forced him to smile; but in general he was looking grave. She wished he could love a ballroom better, and could like Frank Churchill better. – He seemed often observing her. She must not flatter herself that he thought of her dancing, but if he were criticising her behaviour she did not feel afraid.

Given its context and the sparsity of judgement about Mr Knightley's appearance hitherto, this passage has an impact that must be universally felt. A closer look clearly repays attention. Emma is seeing Mr Knightley in a new way: as a handsome man as well as an old friend and a familiar household presence. Accordingly, to her habitually acute consciousness of his opinion of her behaviour, she adds willy-nilly a kind of half-wish that he observe her dancing – i.e. her as a young woman. It is a revealing moment, although Emma, of course, does not realize yet quite what it reveals.

Mr Knightley goes on to fulfil these newly roused expectations in every respect. His rescue of Harriet is not only morally fine but also 'his dancing proved to be just what she had believed it, extremely good'. And the chapter comes to its fitting close with an exchange between the two principals which is both moving and provoking:

> 'Whom are you going to dance with?' asked Mr Knightley.
> She hesitated a moment, and then replied, 'With you, if you will ask me.'
> 'Will you?' said he, offering his hand.
> 'Indeed I will. You have shown that you can dance, and you know we are not really so much brother and sister as to make it at all improper.'
> 'Brother and sister! no, indeed.'

This new sequence receives speedy confirmation in one of Jane Austen's most delicate hints. The scene in Chapter 40 of Harriet's confession and destruction of her *Most precious treasures* and the following extragavance of misunderstanding as to whom she now loves is so extraordinarily funny that an important detail of Emma's response might easily be missed. The most valuable of the Elton relics is an old pencil stub. Harriet had secreted it during a conversation on spruce beer, and tries to remind her friend of the occasion:

> '... I kept my eye on it; and, as soon as I dared, caught it up, and never parted with it again from that moment.'
> 'I do remember it,' cried Emma; 'I perfectly remember it. – Talking about spruce beer. – Oh! yes – Mr Knightley and I both saying we liked it, and Mr Elton's seeming resolved to learn to like it too. I perfectly remember it. – Stop; Mr Knightley was standing just here, was not he? – I have an idea that he was standing just here.'
> 'Ah! I do not know. I cannot recollect. – It is very odd, but I cannot recollect – Mr Elton was sitting here ...'

There can be no doubt now of the force of Mr Knightley's presence for Emma.

The Box Hill episode may be the climax of Emma's deviation. But the immediate result of her consequent repentance is almost – not quite – the culminating point of her fresh awareness of Mr Knightley and his of her. That he will respond to her apologetic visit to the Bates's we expect. But there are two aspects of his response that are new and peculiar. When she meets him on her return, he is 'decidedly graver than usual' (Chapter 45). This is to be expected, and it is natural to assume that he has not yet heard of her errand. But he has. Mr Woodhouse says, 'Emma has been to call on Mrs and Miss Bates . . . as I told you before. She is always so attentive to them!' The change which follows in him can only be attributed to his *looking* at her and her at him, and not to any new information:

> Emma's colour was heightened by this unjust praise; and with a smile and shake of the head, which spoke much, she looked at Mr Knightley. – It seemed as if there were an instantaneous impression in her favour, as if his eyes received the truth from hers, and all that passed of good in her feelings were at once caught and honoured. – He looked at her with a glow of regard.

This is a familiar and piquant situation: a highly articulate verbal art concerning itself with highly articulate people who are usually character-ized particularly through their clear speech finds its climactic issue in a communication that has, and needs, no words. And it is not left there. Mr Knightley and Emma continue to act on instinct and through the senses. As look is succeeded by touch, the prose rhythm imitates the hesitancy of the moment:

> She was warmly gratified – and in another moment still more so, by a little movement of more than common friendliness on his part. He took her hand; – whether she had not herself made the first motion, she could not say – she might, perhaps, have rather offered it – but he took her hand, pressed it, and certainly was on the point of carrying it to his lips – when, from some fancy or other, he suddenly let it go.

Readers may, perhaps, have noticed how full of meaning handshakes are in the novel. This is the last and most significant of a series. But it is not – as it might have been in a lesser work – the immediate signal for the happy finale. Mr Knightley is still too reticent to proceed with his kiss; Emma is confused as to why; Mr Woodhouse, of course, notices nothing; and the action subsides into the usual with Emma's swift regret at not having been able to have a good *talk* about Jane Fairfax. She still, unlike the reader, does not know where she is headed.

We have not long to wait, but a difficult course has to be pursued. All the misunderstandings, save one, are dispelled in a domino effect (the toppling of one causes the others to fall in sequence). Emma is not, to everyone's surprise, dismayed on hearing of Frank's engagement. Instead she generously understands and forgives Jane Fairfax's former rebuffs, and begins to worry furiously about the effect on Harriet. This begins a kind of *reprise* of the Elton affair. But Harriet's revelation of her love for one who is 'five hundred million times more above me than the other' (Chapter 47) provokes a far more dramatic variation. Emma has been guilty of match-making, but not really culpable in the reader's eyes because of the strength of the evidence for Frank's having been the object. The final realization of her own feelings: 'It darted through her, with the speed of an arrow, that Mr Knightley must marry no one but herself!' cannot now be the occasion for the happiness we might have expected. Instead there follows the most rigorous self-reproach:

> She saw it all with a clearness which had never blessed her before. How improperly had she been acting by Harriet! How inconsiderate, how indelicate, how irrational, how unfeeling had been her conduct! What blindness, what madness, had led her on! It struck her with dreadful force ...

Emma is admirable here in her decision – in spite of her own feelings at last being engaged – to be kind and just to Harriet. Her thoughts are in the same clear, lucid vein as over her former mistakes, though now far more than her self-esteem is threatened. She achieves a novel 'resolution to sit and endure' a situation entirely revealed and entirely repulsive. She has never 'really cared' for Frank at all; it should always have been – has always been, if she had but realized it – Mr Knightley; and she has actively 'brought evil' on them all, including Mr Knightley:

> She was most sorrowfully indignant; ashamed of every sensation but the one revealed to her – her affection for Mr Knightley. – Every other part of her mind was disgusting.

What if Jane Austen had decided to end the novel here? But the idea is inconceivable, for the harder Emma is on herself the better we like her, and the less we agree with her. For we, of course, know more than she does. And we are pleased to witness her creation of her final misunderstanding: 'She had no hope ... that he could have that sort of affection for herself which was now in question' – and her final reversion, this time charming rather than complacent, into her first delusion

> Marriage, in fact, would not do for her. It would be incompatible with what she owed to her father, and with what she felt for him. Nothing should separate her from her father. She would not marry, even if she were asked by Mr Knightley.
>
> (Chapter 48)

It is always an amiable fault in her to get carried away with an idea; and now Mr Woodhouse joins little Henry in the ranks of the red herring. Gloom for Emma, happy anticipation for us.

There follows the comic dance of the proposal in Chapter 49. The setting this time is a fine day in early summer. The scene is out of doors but at home. Mr Knightley's reappearance rightly promises the long awaited happy outcome. But the initial misunderstandings are not only a pleasing tease but a forceful reminder of the importance of catching the right moment or losing it for ever. Mutual delicacy almost results in stalemate. Mr Knightley at first gravely skirts around the subject of Frank, now 'a disgrace to the name of man'. But on hearing Emma's difficult but resolute speaking out to the effect that she has 'never been at all attached to the person we are speaking of', he cheers up wonderfully and decides that he 'may have under-rated him' and that Frank 'may yet turn out well'. However, his new manner only serves to raise another obstacle: Emma fears in turn to hear the name of Harriet and quickly rebuffs *his* new determination to speak out. He is mortified, and deadlock almost reached. It is – and this is important – her sense of duty, a result of her genuine self-reproach, that gives her the determination not to go into her father's house and to hear, with however much pain, what he has to say. Naturally what he has to say is not at all painful. And surely Jane Austen's often quoted reticence: 'What did she say? – Just what she ought, of course. A lady always does', has the effect of avoiding redundancy rather than inhibiting feeling. The chapter ends with Mr Knightley: '. . . if he could have thought of Frank Churchill then, he might have deemed him a very good sort of fellow'.

It remains only to return Harriet to Robert Martin at last; to order and reassert feelings all round, including those of the vulgar and envious Mrs Elton; and to cope considerately with the inert selfishness of Mr Woodhouse. This last is achieved with fine insouciant arbitrariness on Jane Austen's part by the invention of the poultry raid. The ending of the love-story is of course the final union of good sense and delicate feeling, the triumph of the moral norm. But – and this is where the conclusion of *Emma* differs from the snappy comprehensive resolutions so often found in novels – society and most of the characters remain their dull and mediocre selves. The conclusion is comparatively long, dramatic, and illustrative. Jane Austen is a very moving comic writer. But she is also a realist.

III Persuasion

1 Autumnal

It is generally true that, when dealing with masterpieces, an enthusiast will prefer the one he has last encountered. In an extreme case the Wagnerian will tell you one week that *Tristan und Isolde* is the greatest work; the next that *Die Meistersinger* is to be preferred; and the next that, after all, *Parsifal* is supreme. And so on with various artists and various arts. This desert island discery is fun, but it is hardly criticism. Leaving aside for the present purposes the considerable claims of *Pride and Prejudice* (perhaps Jane Austen's own favourite) and *Mansfield Park*, the reader of *Emma* who goes on to *Persuasion* will perhaps be most forcibly struck by the important developments that exist within a fundamental similarity. Jane Austen is often thought of as a writer of more or less excellent variations on a single theme. The fragment called *Sanditon* is occasionally proffered, rather wistfully, as evidence of the kind of 'new departure' so beloved by modern critics. But *Persuasion* itself is surely enough to prove that Jane Austen's creative intelligence did not mark time. It is not better than *Emma*; it is different.

This difference is most obvious in the nature of the central couple. No discussion of *Emma* is complete without quoting Jane Austen's remark that 'I am going to take a heroine whom no one but myself will much like', but a similarly cunning pre-emptive defence of *Persuasion* is a little less well known. In a letter to her niece, Fanny Knight, she says: '... pictures of perfection as you know make me sick & wicked ... You may *perhaps* like the Heroine, as she is almost too good for me' (*Letters*, pp. 486–7). It is in fact extremely rare to find anyone who is put off by Anne Elliot's virtues. Why not?

The first reason, as we might expect, lies deep in the prose. Jane Austen does not overtly criticize Anne as she does Emma – the narrator's voice is full of praise, and unfavourable opinions are left for fools to voice. Nor does she show Anne behaving in a fashion either ridiculous or culpable. But she does quite frequently make small and affectionate jokes about her which help to dispel any image of a plaster saint for whom the reader would at best feel a bored respect. This realism affirms goodness but treats it humorously or critically when appropriate – much as one might treat an admired friend. A few examples. When (Chapter 5) the Crofts are to inspect Kellynch with a view to renting it, 'Anne found it most natural to ... keep out of the way till all was over; when she found it most natural to be sorry that she had missed the opportunity of seeing them.' The repetition here alerts us to the amusing irrationality. More seriously, when Mary with her usual relentless stupidity reports Captain Wentworth's opinion that Anne is 'altered beyond his knowledge' (Chapter 7) we expect shock and chagrin and a subsequent Christian resignation. Yet surely Anne is shown as straining her virtues to a point which would become painful or even neurotic in a less stable personality when she reflects on his words:

> Yet she soon began to rejoice that she had heard them. They were of sobering tendency; they allayed agitation; they composed, and consequently must make her happier.

This 'must' must come from the character, not the author. And the strain of guileless idealism in Anne appears quite often. Her reaction to the idea of the lessons in human nature available to nurses is characteristic:

> '... What instances must pass before them of ardent, disinterested, self-denying attachment, of heroism, fortitude, patience, resignation – of all the conflicts and all the sacrifices that ennoble us most. A sick chamber may often furnish the worth of volumes.'

But Mrs Smith quickly supplies the necessary corrective:

> '... I fear its lessons are not often in the elevated style you describe. Here and there, human nature may be great in times of trial, but generally speaking it is its weakness and not its strength that appears in a sick chamber; it is selfishness and impatience rather than generosity and fortitude, that one hears of.'   (Chapter 17)

On a happier note, Jane Austen writes with quite explicit teasing about Anne's feelings when she is at last assured of Wentworth's reawakened love for her:

> Prettier musings of high-wrought love and eternal constancy, could never have passed along the streets of Bath, than Anne was sporting with from Camden-place to Westgate-buildings. It was almost enough to spread purification and perfume all the way.   (Chapter 21)

Appropriate for a city full of all kinds of disease; and perhaps also an oblique comment on the novel itself.

The reader will have noticed many more such touches. The second and more important reason for not finding the hero and heroine intolerable, or not finding in them a mere re-working of Mr Knightley and Emma, lies in the whole conception of the couple and indeed in the shape of the action. There are two contrasting elements held in a uniquely happy conjunction. First, their ages are close and Anne at twenty-seven is, of course, significantly older than most heroines in a comedy of marriage – the Musgrove sisters are the obvious comparison held up in the novel. And Anne is seen as a conscientiously functioning aunt, not, like Emma, a largely theoretical one. Her maturity at least matches that of her lover, and if either deviates from good sense and delicate feeling it is Wentworth – but more of that later. Parts of the book thus acquire that peculiar feeling best described by the frequently used adjective 'autumnal'. Many readers quite naturally feel inclined to associate this with the author's declining health, the prelude to her intolerably early death. But second, in elegant and invigorating counterpoint, there is a freedom, ease, fresh-ness, liberality and vigour deriving largely from the victorious Captain Wentworth but associated with the Navy and its social impact generally. (For a brilliantly suggestive account of Jane Austen's response to this and other aspects of Regency Modernity the interested reader should turn to Q. D. Leavis's essay 'Jane Austen – Novelist of a Changing Society' in her *Collected Essays*, Vol. 1, 1983.)

The 'autumnal' setting is established very early on. A few paragraphs into the book we learn that:

A few years before, Anne Elliot had been a very pretty girl, but her bloom had vanished early; and as even in its height, her father had found little to admire in her, (so totally different were her delicate features and mild dark eyes with his own); there could be nothing in them now that she was faded and thin, to excite his esteem.

This is very emphatic: the bloom 'vanished', and 'delicate' and 'mild' moving into 'faded and thin'. There seems little to hope for even when we know that there will be. Yet the ensuing description of the older but as yet undamaged Elizabeth sets up some new possibilities:

It sometimes happens, that a woman is handsomer at twenty-nine than she was ten years before; and, generally speaking, if there has been neither ill health nor anxiety, it is a time of life at which scarcely any charm is lost.

There is an unstated implication, a promise clear to every reader of novels, that a new bloom will happen for Anne: that while she finds fresh life, Elizabeth will wither. It is interesting to compare this with the more overtly striven-for subtleties of F. Scott Fitzgerald on the same subject in *Tender is the Night*:

... whereas a girl of nineteen draws her confidence from the surfeit of attention, a woman of twenty-nine is nourished on subtler stuff... Happily she does not seem, in either case, to anticipate the subsequent years when her insight will be blurred by panic, by the fear of stopping or the fear of going on. But on the landings of nineteen or twenty-nine she is pretty sure that there are no bears in the hall.

Plenty of bears for the arrogant Elizabeth; none for her delicate and withdrawing sister.

But there is more to the initial melancholy than the basic facts of the situation. Anne's experience in the early part of the novel is all to do with her acceptance of the secondary role of sensitive servant to her moral and spiritual inferiors ('she was only Anne'), with breaking up and moving away, and with the near onset of the winter of 1814. This experience is often echoed in the tone of the prose; and most powerfully perhaps in an unusually long poetical passage which surpasses, I think, the more celebrated earlier description of Lyme. At the beginning of the second volume Anne is left alone with her thoughts (a rare occasion, incidentally, in that oddly crowded society) prior to leaving Uppercross:

> A few months hence, and the room now so deserted, occupied but by her silent, pensive self, might be filled again with all that was happy and gay, all that was glowing and bright in prosperous love, all that was most unlike Anne Elliot!
>
> An hour's complete leisure for such reflections as these, on a dark November day, a small thick rain almost blotting out the very few objects ever to be discerned from the windows, was enough to make the sound of Lady Russell's carriage exceedingly welcome; and yet, though desirous to be gone, she could not quit the mansion-house, or look an adieu to the cottage, with its black, dripping, and comfortless veranda, or even notice through the misty glasses the last humble tenements of the village, without a saddened heart. – Scenes had passed in Uppercross, which made it precious. It stood the record of many sensations of pain, once severe, but now softened; and of some instances of relenting feeling, some breathings of friendship and reconciliation, which could never be looked for again, and which could never cease to be dear. She left it all behind her; all but the recollection that such things had been. (Chapter 13)

Part of the effect of this is due to its contrast with the usually brisk pace of Jane Austen's narrative. It is a moment of relative stillness, dwelling on feeling. Part is due to the predominance of melancholy words which in the first paragraph are balanced by 'happy ... gay ... glowing', etc., but in the second only by the appropriately tentative feel of 'softened ... relenting ... breathings', etc. But most is due to the way in which nature is seen to co-operate with feeling, and vice-versa. Darkness and drizzle are very much to the point (compare the use of seasons in *Emma*, though Emma never has such thoughts) and Anne's view of the scene is coloured by her emotions – the veranda which is now so dreary, for example, was first viewed cheerfully as a 'prettiness' belonging to the Cottage.

This is a powerful summation of the tone set by Anne for the first half of the novel. Its tenderness, if not its sadness, is to remain associated with her. But it is also, with its characteristic counter indications, a prelude to the upswing which gradually follows. This heroine needs more than Emma's youthful good night's sleep to restore her happiness; but the happiness is on its way in the form, of course, of Captain Wentworth. What about him?

2 Captain Wentworth

I have heard it objected that Wentworth, in common with his fellow officers, does not swear enough to be a successful naval commander. This is not so fatuous as it sounds, because one of his important characteristics is, as I have mentioned, to impart a new vigour and practical alacrity into the desiccated, pompous and hollow world of the Elliots. He is not only, as is often fondly surmised, Jane Austen's affectionate tribute to her distinguished brothers (Admiral of the Fleet Sir Francis Austen, K.C.B. incidentally probably did not swear much either, being noted for his piety) but also far closer than others to the dashing hero expected in novels. He is in considerable contrast to Mr Knightley and to Edmund Bertram in *Mansfield Park* in being an outsider with a career to make, and one of the flower of that victorious military generation which with equal gallantry and patience destroyed and utterly humiliated the greatest alien despotism ever, till then, to threaten England. He might, therefore, be allowed a little freedom in his language. Indeed his conduct with the Musgrove girls is, as he later acknowledges, somewhat irresponsible. And even Sir Walter Elliot, that connoisseur of the superficial, is rather abashed by good looks so very evident that they do not need to be gradually realized, as are Mr Knightley's by Emma.

However, the real reason why *Persuasion* offers no help to a compiler of oaths designed to terrify and compel early nineteenth-century sailors is, of course, that Wentworth is experienced by the reader through the sensibility of two elegant women (author and heroine) whose interest in language is more sophisticated and rigorous than that which would be satisfied by a merely surface naturalism. However striking and brave Wentworth may be, and whatever he might be supposed to say aboard the *Asp* or the *Laconia*, we are interested in him as a man of good sense and good feeling, as 'manly' in the best sense of that unfortunately outmoded word. His qualities are most dramatically brought out in the purposeful sequence of encounters with Anne which, again like and unlike those in *Emma*, awaken and rearrange feelings latent or previously existent. But in this novel it is the man experienced rather than the woman experiencing whose best qualities have to be redeemed and brought into line with a norm of excellence which conveys the main import of the book and stands as the chief (not the only) contrast to a surrounding fatuity and spiritual shabbiness. This technical point is both important and easy to grasp. Whereas in *Emma*, through Emma, the 'centre of consciousness' is manifestly and deliberately faulty and perverse, in *Persuasion* it is, through Anne, almost entirely correct *if* we allow for her shyness and her love for Wentworth. Both Mr Knightley and Wentworth are given their moments of direct vision (Chapter 41 and 19 respectively) but the tone of the novels is determined by the nature of their heroines.

In Chapter 3 we are treated to a typical scene at Kellynch where the possibility of Admiral Croft's tenancy is comically discussed:

> 'And who is Admiral Croft?' was Sir Walter's cold suspicious enquiry.
>
> Mr Shepherd answered for his being of a gentleman's family, and mentioned a place; and Anne, after the little pause which followed, added –
>
> 'He is a rear admiral of the white. He was in the Trafalgar action, and has been in the East Indies since; he has been stationed there, I believe, several years.'
>
> 'Then I take it for granted,' observed Sir Walter, 'that his face is about as orange as the cuffs and capes of my livery.'

Anne is, surprisingly, a reader of naval intelligence, which Louisa and Henrietta Musgrove later, unsurprisingly, become. But we are not left long in doubt as to why. The name of Wentworth is mentioned and contemptuously dismissed as 'nothing to do with the Strafford family' (the Earls thereof had been Wentworths) and Anne is able to resort to her 'favourite grove' and say, 'with a gentle sigh, "a few months more and *he*, perhaps, may be walking here."' End of chapter. But the interest thus sparked off is immediately satisfied by the opening of the next (chapter divisions are often a source of pleasure in Jane Austen): '*He* was not Mr Wentworth, the former curate of Monkford, however suspicious appearances may be, but a captain Frederick Wentworth ...' This playfulness on the part of the author leads into an explanation and then into the main action. But the second little shock applied is still prior to the entry of the hero. The extent to which anything to do with Captain Wentworth is a matter of intense interest and intense trepidation to Anne has been well established by the time that she meets the Crofts in Chapter 6. It is, therefore, no surprise that Jane Austen uses the rather new word 'electrified' to describe her response to Mrs Croft's remark: 'It was you and not your sister, I find, that my brother had the pleasure of being acquainted with, when he was in this country.' We are already on the knife edge of fearful emotion which characterizes these sudden, casual, attacks on Anne's security. Here 'she had outlived the age of blushing; but the age of emotion she certainly had not', and so the ensuing: 'Perhaps you may not have heard that he is married', is a severe cut, quickly, as usual, blunted by the realization that the curate and not the captain is in question. Jane Austen ruthlessly *maintains* this kind of pressure – as every reader will remember. Anne's experience has a kind of day-to-day vulnerability which gives the book its special depth. *Persuasion* becomes a desperate cliffhanger of the finer sensibilities.

It would be tedious to note every detail of the sequence thus established. It is clear as well as subtle and forms the core of the narrative. Through it, however, there emerge for the reader some characteristics of Wentworth which though on the whole amiable are seen by Anne, normally so discriminating, in an entirely uncritical manner. We have the fair advantage of not being in love with him. Thus, for example, although his manners and his speech can, and eventually do, come up to the highest standard, we are forced to realize that his beautiful masculine spontaneity has potential drawbacks. Although his naval character does not – in the complex comparisons which are constantly being made – run to the simple bluffness of feeling exhibited by the loveable Admiral Croft, nor to the eventually weak bookishness of a practical man in retreat shown in Captain Benwick, Wentworth is boyish in a way that could be damaging. Compared with Mr Knightley, Mr Darcy, or even to the 'bad' hero Henry Crawford in *Mansfield Park*, he is really rather naïf: which no doubt is the result of the verisimilitude usually achieved by Jane Austen. An incident in Chapter 9 illustrates this well. The scene is highly charged and an important beginning of his reconciliation with Anne. The 'remarkable stout, forward' infant Walter Musgrove has climbed on to Anne's back; she remonstrates with the little beast; Charles Hayter remonstrates:

But not a bit did Walter stir.

In another moment, however, she found herself in the state of being released from him; some one was taking him from her, though he had bent down her head so much, that his little sturdy hands were unfastened from around her neck, and he was resolutely borne away, before she knew that Captain Wentworth had done it.

Her sensations on the discovery made her perfectly speechless. She could not even thank him.

This is admirable and done with great delicacy and tact. We are reminded of the quality of swift, uncomplicated, intelligent action that so much distinguishes Mr Knightley and Emma when in concert. But its really distinguishing feature is that of silence. Wentworth acts excellently on impulse but he does not talk – indeed he declines speech. This is, of course, highly significant in a novel by Jane Austen.

Not that Wentworth is dumb. During the celebrated 'hedge-row' scene in Chapter 10 he is impressed by Louisa's girlish eloquence about her own decisiveness and passionate nature:

> 'If I loved a man, as she loves the Admiral, I would be always with him, nothing should ever separate us, and I would rather be overturned by him, than driven safely by any body else.'
> It was spoken with enthusiasm.
> 'Had you?' cried he, catching the same tone; 'I honour you!'

A sensible man would not so easily catch his tone from a girl who is unlikely to be capable, as is Mrs Croft, of correcting her husband's driving. It is a defect in judgement which Jane Austen further dramatizes in his first long speech shortly afterwards in which he both goes too far in his 'earnest' admiration of Louisa, and produces a rather embarrassing facetious allegory on a hazel-nut. Here he resembles Frank Churchill rather than Mr Knightley. Indeed, the whole of his behaviour in lingering among the female flatteries and charms of Uppercross while he should be paying a visit to his newly married brother would surely provoke a rebuke from the latter. And, if this judgement is felt to be unduly severe, we should note that when he does distinguish himself in this chapter it is again in silence. He determines that Anne shall have a lift in the Admiral's gig and acts with characteristic firmness:

> ... Captain Wentworth, without saying a word, turned to her, and quietly obliged her to be assisted into the carriage.
> Yes, – he had done it. She was in the carriage, and felt that he had placed her there, that his will and his hands had done it, that she owed it to his perception of her fatigue, and his resolution to give her rest.

It remains for the Admiral to round off our sense of the possible pleasant obtuseness of men of action and of the mediocrity of what Wentworth for the moment so admires:

> 'I wish Frederick would spread a little more canvas, and bring us home one of these young ladies to Kellynch. Then, there would always be company for them. – And very nice young ladies they both are; I hardly know one from the other.'

The Cobb catastrophe in Chapter 12 is, of course, the moment when Wentworth begins to learn to distinguish, if not Louisa from Henrietta, at least Anne from them and from everyone else. It is one of those typical occasions in Jane Austen where everybody acts precisely in character and to the reader's delight (Charles Musgrove comes off surprisingly well). But there is a telling variation. We have just heard from Captain Harville of Wentworth's noble behaviour towards Benwick in consoling the latter on the death of his fiancée; how he 'wrote up for leave of absence ... travelled night and day ... and never left the poor fellow for a week'. Jane Austen would have known, and would have expected her contemporaries to know, what an extraordinary sacrifice this action was. The modern reader can get a glimpse of it by comparing a speech about shore leave attributed to Admiral Lord Collingwood in Vigny's *Servitude et Grandeur Militaires* (1835). To his French prisoner aboard his flag ship he says:

'You have only been a prisoner for a month ... but I have been one for thirty-three years. Yes, my friend, I am the sea's prisoner; it hems me in on every side; always waves and more waves. I hear and see nothing else ... I have been so little in England, that I know her only from the map. My country is an ideal ... which I serve as a slave ...'

Lord Collingwood is resigned to being a merely theoretical presence to his family. The sailors in *Persuasion* are happier, but they too speak with emphasis on the subject. We are therefore exceptionally predisposed in Wentworth's favour when Lousia falls:

'She is dead! she is dead!' screamed Mary ... in another moment, Henrietta, sinking under the conviction, lost her senses too ...

'Is there no one to help me?' were the first words which burst from Captain Wentworth, in a tone of despair, and as if all his own strength were gone.

'Go to him, go to him,' cried Anne ...

And Anne takes charge of the situation.

... every thing was done that Anne had prompted, but in vain; while Captain Wentworth, staggering against the wall for his support, exclaimed in the bitterest agony,

'Oh God! her father and mother!'

'A surgeon!' said Anne.

Soon, of course, he recovers his nerve. But is it not surprising that in a society supposedly dominated in practical matters by the male we have, besides three women in various states of collapse, two experienced opponents of Napoleon and a young Squire dependent on the clear-headedness of a retiring young woman? The effect would be ludicrous were it not for its naturalness. But the fact that Wentworth is surpassed in his own *forte* by the heroine should ensure that we take a more critical attitude towards him than she is capable of. Which is perhaps just as well, because the novel is about love as well as discrimination. And Wentworth is perfectly able to learn: from 'she was only Anne' we now pass to his 'no one so proper, so capable as Anne!' Amongst these and other indications of reawakened regard, Volume 1 ends. The indications of 'friendship and reconciliation' in Anne's ensuing autumnal reflections are stronger than she can allow herself to recognize.

One of the things that distinguishes this novel from *Emma* in particular is the emphasis on change of place. Taking up a theme from *Mansfield Park*, Jane Austen constantly stresses the self-absorption characteristic of little communities. Amongst them Anne is a lonely and sympathetic traveller. Her sympathies are hard put to it in Bath, an odious city whose impact seems to resemble that of modern London or New York, and on which all the pettinesses and some of the virtues of Kellynch, Uppercross and Lyme eventually converge. But here, at least, Wentworth's real qualities can shine as they should.

First Anne is given a charming little pre-vision of what it might be like to be married to a Navy man. Her walk with Admiral Croft following his astute piece of art criticism ('I wonder where that boat was built! ... I would not venture over a horsepond in it') is delightful in itself besides conveying the news that Wentworth is free from Louisa and apparently without regret. Then, when he almost immediately appears, she, so accustomed to being routed by apprehension and embarrassment in his company, is now able to notice that he too is overcome with confusion – so different from his previous self-confidence, and so much more attractive. She is the 'winner', as it were, in their encounter at Molland's. The stage is set for the concert in Chapter 20, the turning-point of the sequence.

The charged poignancy of this episode will provoke the admiration of every reader: correspondingly it requires little comment. Anne's triumph is total – so total that it convinces even her. 'He must love her.' However, there are two important features which reinforce its strength, and both rely on and modify what has gone before. The first is that it is left to Anne to take the initiative. In spite of the 'formidable father and sister in the background' in all their daunting frigidity it is her 'gentle "How do you do?"' which allows, or even compels, the newly diffident Captain to talk to her. Then, though, it is his turn. Their conversation, 'exquisite, though agitated' as it is, shows him for the first time to be as accomplished in speech and in the analysis of himself and others as he has been in most of his actions. In a tense and embarrassing situation he talks extremely well. On the new and surprising lovers:

'I confess that I do think there is a disparity, too great a disparity, and in a point no less essential than mind. – I regard Louisa Musgrove as a very amiable, sweet-tempered girl, and not deficient in understanding; but Benwick is something more. He is a clever man, a reading man – and I confess that I do consider his attaching himself to her, with some surprise. Had it been the effect of gratitude, that he learnt to love her, because he believed her to be preferring him, it would have been another thing.'

Precisely – if only we choose with Anne to gloss over his recent admiration of Louisa's firm character. On himself:

'I had been too deeply concerned in the mischief to be soon at peace. It had been my doing – solely mine. She would not have been obstinate if I had not been weak.'

Even more precisely. This new lucidity and elegance, compromised as it is, begins to convince us that he really is worthy of Anne. In fact he can scarcely keep off the welcome and painfully sensitive subjects of parental kindness and constancy in love. And this new mental distinction does not at all detract from his physical glamour. It is now that Sir Walter is moved to his tribute of 'a well-looking man ... a very well-looking man' – more than which could hardly be said.

The suspense of who feels what for whom is now resolved. It is replaced by the less weighty but equally urgent question of how these feelings are to come out. The reader can feel nothing but pleasure at Anne's new anxieties:

How was such jealousy [of Mr Elliot] to be quieted? How was the truth to reach him? How, in all the peculiar disadvantages of their respective situations, would he ever learn her real sentiments?

We may remember similar problems from *Emma*. That they exercised Jane Austen as well as her heroine can be seen by comparing the cancelled Chapter 22 with its more successful substitutes. The controlled chaos of the arrival of Charles and Mary is pleasant and characteristic. Elizabeth's barely verbalized interior monologue about how she can deal with the Musgrove invasion is a finely comic example of the novelist's continued creative experimentation in presenting the mind working:

'Old fashioned notions – country hospitality – we do not profess to give dinners – few people in Bath do – Lady Alicia never does; did not even ask her own sister's family, though they were here a month: and I dare say it would be very inconvenient to Mrs Musgrove – put her quite out of her way. I am sure she would rather not come – she cannot feel easy with us. I will ask them all for an evening; that will be much better – that will be a novelty and a treat. They have not seen two such drawing rooms before.'

And the meeting at the White Hart with all its tensions of meaning and misunderstanding – Anne's and Wentworth's half-conversation, Elizabeth's chilling invitation, Mary's foolishness, Wentworth's well-bred contempt – is Jane Austen at her finest. But all of it leads up to Anne's vital statement about constancy (of which more later), and its result in Wentworth's letter. This, in spite of the inevitability of something of the sort, is nevertheless stunning in its effect because of its having been written *au courant* with the preceding overheard conversation, and therefore assuming the character of a dramatic commentary on it. Another original effect – but one which also recalls Jane Austen's lifelong interest in the epistolary novel. Wentworth is now displaying all the openness which could be desired. He speaks out (as it were) in response to Anne's speaking out. All that remains for him to do in order fully to satisfy the examiners is to complete his self-analysis. He does it handsomely, and concludes:

> '... I was proud, too proud to ask again. I did not understand you. I shut my eyes, and would not understand you, or do you justice. This is a recollection which ought to make me forgive every one sooner than myself ... I have been used to the gratification of believing myself to earn every blessing that I enjoyed ... Like other great men under reverses ... I must endeavour to subdue my mind to my fortune. I must learn to brook being happier than I deserve.'   (Chapter 23)

3 Feeling and Language

So far I have discussed aspects of *Persuasion* which must be evident even to the casual reader – otherwise it would be difficult to explain their virtual absence from critical works. They account for much of its power. However, there are other features initially less obvious but nevertheless extremely important in creating the unique 'feel' of the book.

Jane Austen is occasionally accused of being conscious of, and reacting to, something called 'Romanticism'. In fact it seems unlikely that she would – or indeed could – have read some of the writers which the blundering fingers of commonplace literary history mould into a distinct Movement. Keats or Shelley, for example, must for various reasons have been unknown. Yet the much admired description of Lyme and its environs in Chapter 11, in which Jane Austen seems to have forgotten her determination in *Pride and Prejudice* not to be a travel writer, is often cumbered with the adjective 'Wordsworthian':

> ... Charmouth, with its high grounds and extensive sweeps of country, and still more its sweet retired bay, backed by dark cliffs, where fragments of low rock among the sands make it the happiest spot for watching the flow of the tide, for sitting in unwearied contemplation ... above all, Pinny, with its green chasms between romantic rocks, where the scattered forest trees and orchards of luxuriant growth declare that many a generation must have passed away since the first partial falling of the cliff prepared the ground for such a state, where a scene so wonderful and so lovely is exhibited, as may more than equal any of the resembling scenes of the far-famed Isle of Wight ...

This must seem pretty small beer to a race saturated with instant foreign travel. Emma, we should remember, has never seen the sea, though she is rich and lives near London. The passage would seem far less quaint if we substituted the names of some Far Eastern or even Greek places for the familiar English ones. But this is not the point. Compare a few lines from Wordsworth's great poem 'Tintern Abbey':

> ... These beauteous forms,
> Through a long absence, have not been to me
> As is a landscape to a blind man's eye:
> But oft, in lonely rooms, and 'mid the din
> Of towns and cities, I have owed to them,
> In hours of weariness, sensations sweet,
> Felt in the blood, and felt along the heart;
> And passing even into my purer mind,
> With tranquil restoration ...

Wordsworth is not here concerned with the conventional 'unwearied contemplation' of the waves or anything else. He is proposing a language through which it is possible to explore our perception of the world and its possible uses as a power to sustain the spirit. Though the poem was published nearly twenty years before Jane Austen's death the extraordinary phrases 'Felt in the blood, and felt along the heart' (what do they *mean*?) are entirely alien to her kind of writing and her view of the psyche. Admiration of nature was not invented by poets of this period: and her 'green chasms between romantic rocks' and 'orchards of luxuriant growth', etc., are in the dignified, rather generalized manner of the later eighteenth century. Indeed the treatment of Anne's musings in the 'hedge-row' episode in the previous chapter should have told us much. She walks along

... repeating to herself some few of the thousand poetical descriptions extant of autumn, that season of peculiar and inexhaustible influence on the mind of taste and tenderness, that season which has drawn from every poet, worthy of being read, some attempt at description, or some lines of feeling.

But she soon encounters

...large enclosures, where the ploughs at work, and the fresh-made path spoke the farmer, counteracting the sweets of poetical despondence, and meaning to have spring again ...

This, in its function as a tiny proleptic summary of the whole form of the novel, is Jane Austen's own particular type of poetry.

Not, of course, that she was unaware of the great romantic best-sellers of the day. The 'first-rate' Scott and Byron interest Anne as well as Captain Benwick, and their discussion at the end of Chapter 11 is not only about 'how the *Giaour* was to be pronounced'. But the tone is rather one of amusement than of reverence, and subsequent developments bear this out. When Benwick and Louisa have 'fallen in love over poetry' (Chapter 18) we are, in spite of Wentworth's judicious doubts about their mutual suitability, quite prepared to laugh at her hearty brother's baffled description of the formerly resolute girl as a woman of 'sensibility':

'... but she is altered: there is no running or jumping about, no laughing or dancing; it is quite different. If one happens only to shut the door a little hard, she starts and wriggles like a young dab chick in the water; and Benwick sits at her elbow, reading verses, or whispering to her, all day long.' (Chapter 22)

Anne has issued a fruitless warning of the uses of emotional art to Benwick:

... she thought it was the misfortune of poetry, to be seldom safely enjoyed by those who enjoyed it completely; and that the strong feelings which alone could estimate it truly, were the very feelings which ought to taste it but sparingly. (Chapter 11)

There is no reason to suppose that her creator thought differently. At any rate she does not seem to have shared the dismay of some critics that she was living in the 'Romantic Period'.

Nevertheless there is something very distinctive about the language of *Persuasion*. The book is Jane Austen's most overtly emotional work. This is mainly because of the vulnerability of its heroine and her situation on a knife edge, as I have argued. But a certain freedom of emphasis in describing feelings deepens the effect. The language is, comparatively, violent at times – and not just at high points like the fall off the Cobb or the scene at the White Hart. When Emma describes Mr Knightley as 'mad' we are appropriately taken aback by the strength of the word. But it would not stick out anything like so much from the texture of *Persuasion*. Anne is certainly not a 'dab chick'. But she characteristically feels and behaves with extraordinary intensity. Her reaction to the comparatively minor incident of glimpsing Wentworth when at Molland's is described in short phrases:

For a few minutes she saw nothing before her. It was all confusion. She was lost; and when she had scolded back her senses, she found the others still waiting
... (Chapter 19)

This blackout is actually quite realistic, I think; but it does not accord with the effortless self-control usually associated with Jane Austen's protagonists. There is much effort – which is why Wentworth's subsequent lucidity at the concert is seen as so admirable. Here Anne recovers quickly enough but her emotions are represented in a flurry of words:

All the overpowering, blinding, bewildering, first effects of strong surprise were over with her. Still, however, she had enough to feel! It was agitation, pain, pleasure, a something between delight and misery.

In *Emma* such language is reserved for the climaxes of self-reproach. But the reader will recall many other passages of this sort in *Persuasion*. I shall be discussing the explicitness associated with Mrs Smith later: but we should also note that the new men of the Navy are significantly free in feeling. There is not only Admiral Croft's blunt good humour, Benwick's cultivation of sensibility, and Wentworth's initial ease with Louisa and Henrietta and subsequent passion for Anne; even the staid and rational Captain Harville betrays powerful emotion in public, as Anne perceives after his tribute to Wentworth's conduct following Fanny Harville's death: '... he was too much affected to renew the subject – and when he spoke again, it was of something totally different' (Chapter 12). Jane Austen clearly likes this warm forthrightness. What she dislikes must now be considered.

4   Old and New Values

The nature of the judgement on people in *Persuasion* has a very distinctive quality. A quite fresh, sharp dissatisfaction with some of the forms of traditional society which had formerly been at least tolerated by Jane Austen appears side by side with her familiar critique of human vacuity. And this leads both to a reversion to *explicit* judgements in the manner of the earlier novels and to a significant experiment – the result, perhaps, of a new and stronger unease with the less palatable older elements of Regency England.

First, in order to argue this more clearly, I shall consider the context in which it appears: the habitual comic attack on the ordinary weaknesses of mankind. Perennial selfishness and dullness are not spared any more than they are in *Emma*. But they are dramatized with only the usual tolerant acerbity. Mary is a wonderful paradigm of the former. The episode in Chapter 7 when first Charles and then she persuade themselves that they should go out to dinner to see Captain Wentworth, leaving the injured little Charles with Anne, is one of Jane Austen's great comic sequences. First it is: '"Oh, no! as to the leaving the little boy!" – both father and mother were in much too strong and recent alarm to bear the thought ...' Then Charles becomes convinced that it is 'quite a female case', and 'you would not like to leave him yourself, but you see I can be of no use. Anne will send for me if anything is the matter.' Anne is rightly assumed to be the efficient one. Mary does not resent this and probably does not notice it. Instead she generalizes in the manner of a modern 'feminist': 'If there is any thing disagreeable going on, men are always sure to get out of it ... Very unfeeling! I must say it is very unfeeling of him, to be running away from his poor little boy ... How does he know that he is going on well, or that there may not be a sudden change half an hour hence? ... because I am the poor mother, I am not to be allowed to stir ... My being the mother is the very reason why my feelings should not be tried', etc. And after proposing that they all go and leave the boy with the careful Jemima she jumps at Anne's offer (which has its own motive) to stay. Any 'sudden change' is quickly forgotten and off she rushes with the footnote, 'I should not go, you may be sure, if I did not feel at ease about my dear child.' The point about this is its artless hypocrisy. There really is no reason why Mary should stay, but it has to be pretended that there is; she wishes to adhere to the stereotype of the loving mother while doing exactly as she pleases. All very natural, and fairly harmless. How harmless can be appreciated by comparison with a similar piece of comic self-persuasion in Chapter 2 of the much earlier *Sense and Sensibility* where, under the grilling of his mean and rationalizing wife, John Dashwood convinces himself that in place of the gift of £3,000 to his stepmother and her daughters (our heroines) with which he proposes to honour his father's dying wishes it would be more 'decorous' to substitute occasional 'neighbourly acts' – i.e. virtually nothing. This too has as its pretext supposed justice to a child: but its blank nastiness is stark in relation to Mary's mere silliness. Human weaknesses in later Jane Austen tend to be more trivial than sinister – hence the strength of the light in which the artificial coldness and vice of Sir Walter, Elizabeth, and Mr Elliot are later displayed.

The same is true of the treatment of dullness and limitation. It is, as usual, entirely realistic. The Musgrove family are happy and entirely worthy, as we learn in the course of a contrast between the parents and daughters:

> The Musgroves, like their houses, were in a state of alteration, perhaps of improvement. The father and mother were in the old English style, and the young people in the new. Mr and Mrs Musgrove were a very good sort of people; friendly and hospitable, not much educated, and not at all elegant. Their children had more modern minds and manners ... Henrietta and Louisa, young ladies of nineteen and twenty, who had brought from a school at Exeter all the usual stock of accomplishments, and were now, like thousands of other young ladies, living to be fashionable, happy, and merry ... Anne always contemplated them as some of the happiest creatures of her acquaintance; but still, saved as we are all by some comfortable feeling of superiority ... she would not have given up her own more elegant and cultivated mind for all their enjoyments; and she envied them nothing but that seemingly perfect good understanding and agreement together, that good-humoured mutual affection, of which she had known so little herself with either of her sisters.
>
> (Chapter 5)

This is far more genial than is the judgemental manner used about the Elliots. But it is nevertheless a portrait of the most lethal, boring ordinariness. The 'usual stock of accomplishments ... like thousands of other young ladies' – perhaps Admiral Croft is not so far off the mark after all in being unable to tell the sisters apart. And it is in this context, all too reminiscent of Highbury society, by the way, that we should view what is sometimes considered to be a blot on the character of the delightful Miss Austen: her treatment of Mrs Musgrove's delayed laments about the 'thick-headed, unfeeling, unprofitable Dick Musgrove', the memory of whom his ex-Captain's presence revives and who is now called 'poor Richard'. In her commentary the author makes it clear that realism, not comfort, is her aim:

> Captain Wentworth should be allowed some credit for the self-command with which he attended to her large fat sighings over the destiny of a son, whom alive nobody had cared for.
>
> Personal size and mental sorrow have certainly no necessary proportions. A large bulky figure has as good a right to be in deep affliction, as the most graceful set of limbs in the world. But, fair or not fair, there are unbecoming conjunctions, which reason will patronize in vain – which taste cannot tolerate, – which ridicule will seize. (Chapter 8)

Flaubert is celebrated for his remorseless realism, often as though it were something new. Here is his account of a similar loss:

> Long afterwards she learnt the circumstances of Victor's death from the captain of his ship. He had gone down with yellow fever, and they had bled him too much at the hospital. Four doctors had held him at once. He had died straight away, and the chief doctor had said: 'Good! There goes another!' ('A Simple Heart', 1875)

Neither writer seems to me unfeeling. Both dislike cant. And Jane Austen's toughness no doubt has the further function of validating by contrast Anne's habitual tenderness.

Captain Benwick's inconstancy to the memory of Fanny Harville gets similar treatment. It does disturb the deeper natures of Harville and Wentworth; perhaps it should be the target of Lady Russell's stricture on 'characters of fancied enthusiasms and violent agitation' in her praise of Mr Elliot; but we are not invited to feel indignant – only that he is rather shallow, like his Louisa.

It is because of effects like these that Jane Austen is rightly admired for the subtlety and complexity of her judgements in the later novels: particularly adverse judgements. Outright condemnation of people by the narrator in *Emma* is present, but subdued and mixed in with dramatizations of those people's qualities. The strictures on Mr Woodhouse in

Chapter 1, for example, are quickly justified in action. It is left for the characters, in themselves fallible, to issue sweeping accounts of the failings of others – Mr Knightley on Frank Churchill being perhaps the most delightful instance. Mrs Elton is largely condemned out of her own big mouth. And even in the opening of the earlier *Pride and Prejudice* the famous authorial savaging of Mrs Bennet:

> She was a woman of mean understanding, little information, and uncertain temper. When she was discontented she fancied herself nervous. The business of her life was to get her daughters married; its solace was visiting and news.

is preceded by examples of her conversational fatuity. So, to move now to what is new and somewhat disconcerting in *Persuasion*, there is commonly a kind of alarm mixed in with the pleasure of sophisticated readers at the opening account of Sir Walter Elliot. He is allowed no leeway at all. And to remark on the 'Johnsonian' character – the balanced phrases and adjectives – of the heavily satirical first sentences is perhaps often to mask a slight dismay:

> Sir Walter Elliot, of Kellynch-hall, in Somersetshire, was a man who, for his own amusement, never took up any book but the Baronetage; there he found occupation for an idle hour, and consolation in a distressed one; there his faculties were roused into admiration and respect, by contemplating the limited remnant of the earliest patents; there any unwelcome sensations, arising from domestic affairs, changed naturally into pity and contempt, as he turned over the almost endless creations of the last century ...

This is another critique of reading habits. But unlike the account of Harriet's 'mental provision ... for the evening of life' with her book of riddles, or the use of Scott and Byron in Benwick's wooing, its humour is not in the least forgiving. It is followed by a passage in which any kind of humour is unusually absent until the sardonic last sentence:

> Vanity was the beginning and end of Sir Walter Elliot's character; vanity of person and of situation ... Few women could think more of their personal appearance than he did: nor could the valet of any new made lord be more delighted with the place he held in society. He considered the blessing of beauty as inferior only to the blessing of a baronetcy; and the Sir Walter Elliot who united these gifts, was the constant object of his warmest respect and devotion.

Nothing that Sir Walter does or says in the novel softens the force of these strictures. If anything he gets worse, and ends as a 'foolish spendthrift, baronet who had not had principle or sense enough to maintain himself in the situation in which Providence had placed him' and who cannot pay his daughter's dowry because of his selfish habits (Chapter 24); any incipient sympathy the reader may be inclined to feel for such a fictional underdog is checked rigorously by the real lovelessness and careless cruelty he displays towards Anne.

The question therefore arises as to why Jane Austen manifests such unconcealed hostility and contempt towards a person whom she might be expected to regard as at least socially respectable. Partly it is because he is a traitor to his own position in society: a failure as a baronet who, together with his privileges, has responsibilities to his dependents (compare the use of social position by Mr Darcy, or Sir Thomas Bertram in *Mansfield Park*). More interestingly, there does emerge in *Persuasion* a new irritation with some, at least, of the codes which had previously been endorsed. Jane Austen is in no sense revolutionary, but she becomes even more deeply critical. Critical to the extent that she contents herself with a thumbnail sketch of Sir Walter as too obvious a case (not a caricature, I think) to justify a more sustained treatment. He is taken, as it were, for granted, while the deep introspective nature of Anne and the counterpointed freshness of the Navy occupy the centre of the stage.

And this modification of attitude is even more interesting if we focus closely on Mr William Elliot, whose abrupt decline into unambiguous villainy near the end tends to deflect the attention of readers from what he, initially at least, seems to represent. He is, as I have said, a kind of experiment. As Anne's sincere suitor he puts himself above the ruck of triviality and into direct comparison with Wentworth. Lady Russell is by no means infallible, of course: but she might be expected to be an acute judge of a true gentleman, and this is what she thinks:

> Every thing united in him; good understanding, correct opinions, knowledge of the world, and a warm heart. He had strong feelings of family-attachment and family-honour, without pride or weakness; he lived with the liberality of a man of fortune, without display; he judged for himself in every thing essential, without defying public opinion in any point of worldly decorum. He was steady, observant, moderate, candid; never run away with by spirits or by selfishness, which fancied itself strong feeling; and yet, with a sensibility to what was amiable and lovely, and a value for all the felicities of domestic life, which characters of fancied enthusiasm and violent agitation seldom really possess. (Chapter 16)

A paragon. I recently read this passage to an audience familiar with Jane Austen and they agreed that it was an excellent, if perhaps over explicit, description of Mr Knightley. And Anne, in spite of her lingering doubts as to his motives, cannot really disagree with Lady Russell. What a pity it is, then, that the revelations of Mrs Smith so quickly and blackly dismiss Mr Elliot. For what we have is, surely, a potential critique of the traditional gentleman which would have been of profound interest if the exigencies of haste to finish the main story and perhaps of failing health had not forced Jane Austen to abandon it. Mr Elliot could never finally have superseded Wentworth in Anne's affections. The whole structure of the novel tells us that. But he remains a puzzle. If he is present merely as a complication – a traditional stumbling block, a hint at other possibilities, etc. – why is he so developed, so rounded out, so charming? Why the uncharacteristic use of a more or less arbitrary tale of past wickedness which removes the need to explore or explain what is *really* wrong with him – except for the (nonetheless telling) lack of openness which he shares with, for example, the virtuous Jane Fairfax? Why was Jane Austen so interested in the creation of a perfect gentleman who is the absolute reverse of what he seems – and is thus unlike any other of her characters, who signal their true nature to the reader with beautiful reliability? What, finally, were to be, or could have been, his *non-melodramatic* defects? Such questions are only speculative. They leave him a poor fictional second to Henry Crawford in *Mansfield Park*, whose real virtues and enormous charm are ruined by his careless hedonism. But as far as he goes he is thoroughly convincing. Full of Wentworth as she is, Anne is impressed:

... his countenance improved by speaking, and his manners were so exactly what they ought to be, so polished, so easy, so particularly agreeable, that she could compare them in excellence to only one person's manners. They were not the same, but they were, perhaps, equally good. (Chapter 15)

Perhaps we ought to conclude from this that they were better. And where consideration for others is concerned his attitude is placed in contrast to the hollow conventionality of Sir Walter and Elizabeth. When the accident at Lyme is mentioned:

She could only compare Mr Elliot to Lady Russell, in the wish of really comprehending what had passed, and in the degree of concern for what she must have suffered in witnessing it.

Even when they are discussing the ridiculous deferential fuss made by Sir Walter and Elizabeth over the Dalrymples he prefaces his defence of keeping up the connection with some charming good sense:

'My idea of good company, Mr Elliot, is the company of clever, well-informed people, who have a great deal of conversation; that is what I call good company.'
'You are mistaken,' said he gently, 'that is not good company, that is the best. Good company requires only birth, education and manners, and with regard to education is not very nice ... My cousin, Anne, shakes her head. She is not satisfied. She is fastidious. My dear cousin, (sitting down by her) you have a better right to be fastidious than almost any other woman I know; but will it answer? Will it make you happy?' (Chapter 16)

There may be a bit too much oil here, but the argument is not at all silly.

We are left, before the débâcle, only with Anne's lingering disquiet with his seemingly too perfect nature:

> She prized the frank, the open-hearted, the eager character beyond all others. Warmth and enthusiasm did captivate her still ... Mr Elliot was too generally agreeable. (Chapter 17)

Again we regret that Mr Elliot is not allowed to be more than a passing threat: that his polished self, unstained by former crimes, is not allowed to shine in genuine competition with the open-heartedness of the new men. Then we might have seen nearer to the heart of what is being attempted in this part of the novel.

Nevertheless, while this dark experiment is in progress, the pressure to look again at conventional forms becomes even more clear in the open and *bona fide* awfulness of Sir Walter and his eldest daughter in the latter parts of the novel. To add to what is said and seen of them at first we are forced, with pleasure of course, to realize what becomes of them in Bath. This is really humiliating. While at Kellynch Sir Walter is supported by a kind of traditional respect. He has a position, however ill he conducts himself in it. But in Bath he pointedly becomes a kind of nothing – i.e. reveals his true nature. It is often said that Jane Austen never applies external authorial punishments to her bad characters. The only cliffs they step off are the ones they are too stupid or too hardened to recognize as cliffs. The most famous example of this occurs in *Mansfield Park*, when the disgraced Maria Bertram is joined in virtual exile by her hateful Aunt Norris in an establishment '... remote and private, where, shut up together with little society, on one side no affection, on the other, no judgement, it may be reasonably supposed that their tempers became their mutual punishment' (Chapter 48).

But the senior Elliots have an equally grim future, and this is because their particular forms of conventionality can only adapt to change by self-parody. Anne reacts to the 'modern' – in the form of Wentworth – by embracing the 'frank, the open-hearted, the eager' while at the same time retaining her own refinement, elegance and proper pride. By contrast Sir Walter takes pride in what is unworthy. There can be fewer more excruciating amusements in Jane Austen than Anne's introduction to his new establishment:

> Sir Walter had taken a very good house in Camden-place, a lofty, dignified situation, such as becomes a man of consequence ... Anne entered it with a sinking heart ... They had the pleasure of assuring her that Bath more than answered their expectations in every respect. Their house was undoubtedly the best in Camden-place; their drawing-rooms had many decided advantages over all the others which they had either seen or heard of ... Their acquaintance was exceedingly sought after ... (Chapter 15)

The 'best in Camden-place' indeed. Those who have been, and ought to be, nobs have become vulgar snobs. Jane Austen cannot restrain her indignation with her own creations:

> Here were funds of enjoyment! Could Anne wonder that her father and sister were happy? She might not wonder, but she must sigh that her father should feel no degradation in his change; should see nothing to regret in the duties and dignity of the resident land-holder; should find so much to be vain of in the littlenesses of a town; and she must sigh, and smile, and wonder too, as Elizabeth threw open the folding-doors and walked with exultation from one drawing-room to the other, boasting of their space, at the possibility of that woman, who had been mistress of Kellynch Hall, finding extent to be proud of between two walls, perhaps thirty feet asunder.

As we have seen, Jane Austen expects people in positions of superiority to earn their keep by being really superior. And here the minor dignity of a baronet betrays itself into a pretentious sham, amidst – and this is the galling point – a burst of self-applause. What we are really led to hold against Sir Walter is that he will never have even a glimmer of how awful he is. The effect is entirely realistic. One has only to look at contemporary property prices in the stuffy, noisy and gloomy precincts of modern London W.1., S.W.1., S.W.7., etc. – or even Fulham – to realize how little English society has changed. Sir Walter is still perhaps too much of a real Squire to make a pompous and vulgar cult of shooting and hunting in the modern urban rich man's manner, and the pure and demanding vacuity of golf is unavailable to him; but we feel that he would if he could – or rather, if other people did. (It is interesting that sensible men in Jane Austen tend to be indifferent to, for example, shooting birds: Sir Walter makes a fuss about the privileges to be allowed to a tenant, but Admiral Croft, who fought at Trafalgar, 'sometimes took out a gun, but never killed' – and Charles Musgrove is conveniently, at the end, so crazy about guns that he leaves Anne and Wentworth in peace.) One of the numerous passages in the 'radical' Dickens in which he vivaciously denounces the vanity of snobs is concerned with the literal 'littlenesses of a town':

> Mews Street, Grosvenor Square, was not absolutely Grosvenor Square itself, but it was very near it. It was a hideous little street of dead wall, stables, and dunghills ... Yet there were two or three small airless houses at the entrance end ... which went at enormous rents on account of their being abject hangers-on to a fashionable situation; and whenever one of these fearful little coops was to be let (which seldom happened, for they were in great request) the house agent advertised it as a gentlemanly residence in the most aristocratic part of town ... If a gentlemanly residence ... had not been essential to the blood of the Barnacles, this particular branch would have had a pretty wide selection among, let us say, ten thousand houses, offering fifty times the accommodation for a third of the money ... Arthur

Clennam came to a squeezed house, with a ramshackle bowed front, little dingy windows, and a little dark area like a damp waistcoat-pocket, which he found to be number twenty-four ...   (*Little Dorrit*, 1857–8, Chapter 10)

Dickens seems, like us, to associate this kind of thing with the old-fashioned, whereas for the 'conservative' Jane Austen Bath was modern in the wrong way. But her critique is, if anything, more scathing.

Pride in Camden-place is not the end of the Elliots' folly, however. Nor is the idea that Mr Elliot fancies Elizabeth. Nor the blindness to Mrs Clay's insinuating nature. There is something far worse: their behaviour to the innocent Dalrymples. On the arrival of the Dowager Viscountess and her daughter, 'the agony was, how to introduce themselves'.

Anne had never seen her father and sister before in contact with nobility, and she must acknowledge herself disappointed. She had hoped better things from their high ideas of their own situation in life, and was reduced to form a wish which she had never foreseen – a wish that they had more pride ...   (Chapter 16)

Then follows a sequence of gruesome toadying, with characteristically fine comic moments. The point about this is not that the Dalrymples themselves are unworthy – although their title *is* Irish. So far as they exist they are merely commonplace. Jane Austen, like many English novelists before and after her, seems to have been rather hostile to the aristocracy as opposed to her own class, the gentry. The extremely exalted Fitzwilliam Darcy of Pemberley has to undergo some change in character before he can marry Elizabeth Bennet (and vice-versa); his aunt, Lady Catherine, is awful; and we receive a very unpleasant impression of Mrs Churchill in *Emma*. (For a fascinating discussion of this problem, see 'Jane Austen and the Peerage' by Donald J. Greene, reprinted in *Jane Austen: A Collection of Critical Essays*, ed. Ian Watt, Englewood Cliffs, N.J., 1963; for a mere summary of the plot see Andrew H. Wright's essay, '*Persuasion*', in the same volume.) These discriminations are never unimportant, though some modern specialists find them difficult to grasp in the face of the evidence: on the one hand Dr J. Odmark describes Mr Darcy as upper-middle-class, on the other David Monaghan groups Sir Walter with Lady Catherine as 'members of the aristocracy', etc. (how *can* they?). But in *Persuasion* the case is different: while the token aristocrats, the Dalrymples, are, as Anne drastically reflects, 'nothing', and certainly not offensive, the Elliots' pride in them – 'Our cousins in Laura-place' 'Our cousin Lady Dalrymple and Miss Carteret' – is degrading. Especially when it leads to its obverse in the passage already quoted when Sir Walter scorns Mrs Smith – a tactically chosen name if ever there was one. I do not think that Jane Austen abandoned her habitual standards in *Persuasion* in frantic disgust at the older respectability and impulsive greeting of the new. She is much more complicated than that. But there is certainly a novel urgency in the sense, centred in both Sir Walter and Mr Elliot, that hollowness may become compatible with a respectable appearance.

Lady Russell has an important place here: it is not only Anne who manifests the older type of elegance. She is aligned on the side of baronetcy (in theory, at least) and is in favour of the Dalrymple connection. That she is not a woman of very acute judgement is made clear throughout, but that she is a mother to Anne and a person of honesty, warmth and principle is made even clearer. No doubt she too will become a student of the naval gazettes.

Lastly on this subject, another aspect of Bath life provides an even grimmer, though much less certain and emphatic, glimpse of the degradation of the respectable. It is to be noticed in little things as when a chance, or apparently chance, remark of Sir Walter's brings home to us that his vanity, hitherto largely a matter of views on clothes and complexions and a ludicrous plethora of mirrors, is revealed as comprising also a crude sexual complacency:

> 'He had never walked any where arm in arm with Colonel Wallis, (who was a fine military figure, though sandy-haired) without observing that every woman's eye was upon him; every woman's eye was sure to be upon Colonel Wallis.' Modest Sir Walter! He was not allowed to escape, however. IIis daughter and Mrs Clay united in hinting that Colonel Wallis's companion might have as good a figure as Colonel Wallis ... (Chapter 15)

But there is worse. The modern reader may smile at Anne's severity when she reflects that Mr Elliot's mysterious past has included 'Sunday-travelling' – though perhaps he should not, in view of the fact that non-observance of the Sabbath is a recent development. I remember with affection Dorothy Round, the Wimbledon tennis champion of the 1930s, who was famous not only for being a champion but for her refusal to play on Sundays: inconceivable now. But when that past loses its mystery through the fortuitous revelations of Mrs Smith we see, or half see, a world of raffish debauchery for which even the loose set surrounding the Crawfords in *Mansfield Park* has not prepared us. Mrs Smith's narrative is not the only part of the book which shows evidence of a lack of revision. At the end of Chapter 14, for instance, it is unclear who the 'many other persons in Bath' that Anne would rather not see again can possibly be. But it is the worst. As I have argued, it is a pity that Mr Elliot is made quite so bad. He did not have to be, and while this fact strengthens our feeling that Jane Austen was strongly concerned to convey and justify a mistrust of what appears to be estimable, it nevertheless slightly weakens the book. The prose is bald and relatively thin. At times it reads more like some sensational or Gothick novelist of the period than Jane Austen, and might have delighted Catherine Morland:

> Mr Elliot is a man without heart or conscience; a designing, wary, cold-blooded being, who thinks only of himself; who, for his own interest or ease, would be guilty of any cruelty, or any treachery, that could be perpetrated without risk of his general character. He has no feeling for others. Those whom he has been the chief cause of leading into ruin, he can neglect and desert without the smallest compunction. He is totally beyond the reach of any sentiment of justice or compassion. Oh! he is black at heart, hollow and black! (Chapter 21)

'My expressions startle you,' apologizes Mrs Smith. Yes, they do. But not enough, fortunately, seriously to impair the general fineness of the novel. It is noticeable that most readers are content to take Mrs Smith for the purely functional convenience that she is, and to read on without dismay. And a comparable attitude may be adopted to Mrs Clay's faintly implausible elopement to become a kept woman at Mr Elliot's, possibly considerable, expense. For after the collapse of the Elliot respectability there are more interesting and urgent things to attend to.

5 Persuasion and Passivity?

Sometimes one wishes that works of art did not have titles, or that titles did not have their insidious power of directing the attention. For while some are general and neutral (*War and Peace*), some fairly meaningless (*The Winter's Tale*), some unexceptionable (*Emma*, *The Fifth Queen*, *Moby Dick*), and some valuable as a guide (*The Woodlanders*, *The Last Puritan*, *Aaron's Rod*), many are limiting and misleading in making us give undue prominence to a part of a much larger and interesting whole. *Julius Caesar* and *Nostromo* are obvious examples of this last kind; *Pride and Prejudice* probably; *Persuasion* certainly. Of course it was Henry Austen who gave this title to his sister's posthumous novel – which she had earlier referred to as 'The Elliots' – and his choice reflects an intelligent reading. But it is not the only one, and not the best. The trouble is that people tend to concentrate their attention on instances in the novel where people influence themselves or others, and since this frequently happens in life, they can naturally find a lot. This may blind them to a great deal else.

The major example of Lady Russell's prudent advice to the younger Anne, the harm that this, as it happens, has done, and the concluding complicated discussion of the question between Anne Wentworth in Chapter 23 are so important, and so obviously important, that no comment is called for (though it is often supplied). Surely Anne must be right in relieving us of abstract considerations when she remarks, 'It was, perhaps, one of those cases in which advice is good or bad only as the event decides.' Nevertheless it is very well worth noting that the event, having at last decided in favour of happiness, and perhaps made up for the sad waste of neglected years with an access of stable intensity, remains to be waited on. In *Emma* the central couple are to live on in a world where little else has improved. In *Persuasion* this is equally the case. But here there is the important and original addition that the union itself is still threatened by the uncertainty which led to its delay in the first place. There is a slightly worrying, and too little noticed, strain in the triumph of the final words:

... the dread of a future war [was] all that could dim her sunshine. She gloried in being a sailor's wife, but she must pay the tax of quick alarm for belonging to that profession which is, if possible, more distinguished in its domestic virtues than its national importance.

One might speculate that it is our impression, unavailable to heroine or author, of an era of peace after 1815 which leads to the idea that this novel has a perfectly unclouded happy ending. In fact the chanciness of life is still to the fore.

Meanwhile it is also true that 'persuasion' is a key word, though by no means the only one. We can admire the virtuosity with which it is used when, for instance, Anne reflects sadly that:

She was persuaded that under every disadvantage of disapprobation at home, and every anxiety attending his profession ... she should yet have been a happier woman in maintaining the engagement, than she had been in the sacrifice of it
...   (Chapter 4)

Here the word means nearly the opposite of its normal use: Anne has been convinced by subsequent and chance experience rather than by the opinions and predictions of others. She is wise after the event, not prudent before it. And the idea of persuasion does have a habit of cropping up and shouting for attention at significant points. Thus when Wentworth is just turning his bemused interest back to Anne at Lyme, Henrietta, chattering characteristically about her own concerns, remarks with unconscious tactlessness: 'I have always heard of Lady Russell, as a woman of the greatest influence with every body! I always look upon her as able to persuade a person to any thing!' (Chapter 12). Much play with it and its opposite in Louisa is made, and the events after the accident make Anne at least hope at the end of the first volume that 'it could hardly escape him to feel, that a persuadable temper might sometimes be as much in favour of happiness, as a very resolute character'. And so on. After hearing Mrs Smith's revelations and being thus relieved from any temptation offered by Mr Elliot and the deeply pleasing idea entailed of succeeding her mother as the proper Lady Elliot, mistress of Kellynch Hall, Anne sounds the theme in its original form when she shudders at the idea that 'It was just possible that she might have been persuaded by Lady Russell!' In fact the main action of the last part of the book consists in persuading Captain Wentworth out of his new diffidence and his misapprehensions concerning Anne's feelings.

Such patterning is not the mechanical thing it may come to seem under the hands of a commentator. The superb control exercised by the later Jane Austen over her novels, a control at its peak of perfection in *Emma*, may or may not be the result of conscious planning, of 'art'. We can never know. But it clearly is, more importantly, the result of the unremitting pressure to examine dramatically and imaginatively the ideas and perceptions which led to the writing of novels in the first place. The recurrence of the idea of persuasion is thus directly related to the expression of a larger concern: a concern about the proper role of women. Emma, like Elizabeth Bennet, is a lively directrix whose habitual blunders are happily redeemed. Anne suffers in passive and sensitive rectitude. And the objection, like that to Wentworth's failure to swear, can be made that she and her creator are annoying because they think in their limited and society-conditioned way that women are made to suffer and only men to act. That this is a foolish anachronism can be indicated by extending the line of enquiry to such interesting questions as: 'Why doesn't a clever woman like Mrs Clay become a partner in her father's firm?' or 'Can't Mrs Smith pull herself together and sort out her own affairs in the West Indies?' But there is nevertheless a real point lurking somewhere, about which Jane Austen was obviously concerned.

As to actions, I have already noted how crucial Anne's collected behaviour on the Cobb is and how it in effect puts the men to shame. Also that but for her intrepid 'How do you do?' at the concert Wentworth might well have retired from the field for good. Even so it is entirely true that throughout the novel Anne's delicate nature (a feature not entirely incident to maids) and her position as an unmarried younger daughter in that society make her, like Fanny Price in *Mansfield Park*, a person who is played upon by others rather than vice-versa. She is perpetually, consistently and obviously everyone else's patient servant, however contemptible or trivial their demands. Apart from what has been said about this already it is significant that, in a context supplied for us by *Emma*, it is she who during the 'unpremeditated little ball' at Uppercross willingly plays the piano but does not dance. And it is probably no coincidence that with Anne as her heroine Jane Austen makes what is probably her most explicit statement of Christian virtues; of Mrs Smith Anne thinks:

A submissive spirit might be patient, a strong understanding would supply resolution, but here was something more: here was that elasticity of mind, that disposition to be comforted, that power of turning readily from evil to good, and of finding employment which carried her out of herself, which was from Nature alone. It was the choicest gift of Heaven; and Anne viewed her friend as one of those instances in which, by a merciful appointment, it seems designed to counterbalance almost every other want. (Chapter 17)

However, too much emphasis on this aspect of Anne may lead us to miss or ignore a corollary which is equally or even more important. Passive as her behaviour normally is, her mind is quite certainly the best, most lucid and most active in the novel – except, of course, Jane Austen's. Her judgement is constant, forthright and charitably astringent. This could be illustrated over and over again since a great deal, though naturally not all, of what we know about the other characters, their virtues and deficiencies, comes straight from her. Consider the initial characterization of the younger Mr and Mrs Musgrove:

She had no dread of these two months. Mary was not so repulsive and unsisterly as Elizabeth, nor so inaccessible to all influence of hers ... Charles Musgrove was civil and agreeable; in sense and temper he was undoubtedly superior to his wife; but not of powers, or conversation, or grace [to make Anne regret her refusal of him] ... a woman of real understanding might have given more consequence to his character, and more usefulness, rationality, and elegance to his habits and pursuits. As it was, he did nothing with much zeal, but sport; and his time was trifled away, without benefit from books, or any thing else. (Chapter 6)

Far from being the thoughts of a timid and repressed little woman, this is full of a tranquil, lofty and assured confidence which might result in arrogance in a lesser person. The example is particularly apt because it refers, characteristically, to the role and influence of a woman in marriage. It leads us on to the climactic scene in which Anne displays her powers of action and of mind at their best, and in a manner typically hers. Emma's courage and ability to speak out at the right moment leads to her happiness. So does Anne's to hers.

The small gatherings at the White Hart in Chapters 22 and 23 have a typically Austenian ethos. They consist of a group of people with more or less private concerns who are hindered by politeness from expressing them. Really intimate and sensitive matters, especially those concerning the relations of the sexes, cannot come out at all directly. Sociability inhibits expression. The alternative of private meetings is nearly out of the question. Even Mrs Musgrove is reduced to a 'powerful whisper'. Yet the second gathering is better than the first when the entry of Sir Walter and Elizabeth and their invitations petrifies the general chat:

Anne felt an instant oppression, and, wherever she looked, saw symptoms of the same. The comfort, the freedom, the gaiety of the room was over, hushed into cold composure, determined silence, or insipid talk, to meet the heartless elegance of her father and sister.

The Elliots, of course, do not justify the grandeur of their visit by any real benefit conferred, but rather confuse and anger with their tawdry invitation to Elizabeth's 'novelty and … treat'. The second occasion is easier but even then it takes Captain Harville's little smile from his relative retirement by the window to rouse Anne from the 'buzz of words in her ear', her confusion. Then in her debate with him, unaware that she can be overheard by Wentworth, she is able to say directly what she thinks. Naturally in this novel the subject is the nature, position and constancy of men and women. The tone, unlike that of many such debates, is sincere and amiable. In face of Harville's pleasant scepticism Anne states the position of women:

'We live at home, quiet, confined, and our feelings prey upon us. You are forced on exertion … continual occupation and change soon weaken impressions.'

Harville counters that the changeable Benwick has had no such excuse. Men's strong bodies are in analogy with their strong feelings.

'Your feelings may be the strongest,' replied Anne, 'but … ours are the most tender. Man is more robust than woman, but he is not longer-lived …'

What can be learnt from literature? Harville argues justly:

'… let me observe that all histories are against you, all stories, prose and verse … I do not think I ever opened a book in my life which had not something to say upon woman's inconstancy. Songs and proverbs, all talk of woman's fickleness. But perhaps you will say, these were all written by men.'

As I noted earlier, the ball is now even more firmly in the proud lady novelist's court than it had been in the famous passage on novels from *Northanger Abbey*. 'Perhaps I shall,' replies Anne,

'– Yes, yes, if you please, no reference to examples in books. Men have had every advantage of us in telling their own story. Education has been theirs in so much higher a degree; the pen has been in their hands. I will not allow books to prove any thing.'

This is from a book quite determined to 'prove' a good deal. The argument is excellent, if not conclusive. But its complexity is recognized by both parties – again unlike the stridency and foolish arguing for victory which characterizes more common disputes on the topic. Harville answers her attack on education and social conditioning with, 'But how shall we prove any thing?', and Anne states an important agreement:

'We never shall. We never can expect to prove any thing upon such a point. It is a difference of opinion which does not admit of proof. We each begin probably with a little bias towards our own sex, and upon this bias build every circumstance in favour of it which has occurred within our own circle . . .'

The context of this discussion, rational and semi-generalized and proper as it is, is that of great personal feeling – of Anne's moment-to-moment precariousness and of Harville's recent loss. So now it becomes explicitly infused with emotion. Harville speaks with great fervency about his own feelings on being separated from his family by the sea. And Anne responds with something deeply drawn from her experience of a woman's role, and, incidentally, of the genuine opposite to over persuasion:

'God forbid that I should undervalue the warm and faithful feelings of any of my fellow-creatures . . . I believe you equal to every important exertion, and to every domestic forbearance, so long as – if I may be allowed the expression, so long as you have an object. I mean, while the woman you love lives, and lives for you. All the privilege I claim for my own sex (it is not a very enviable one, you need not covet it) is that of loving longest, when existence or when hope is gone.'

She could not immediately have uttered another sentence; her heart was too full, her breath too much oppressed.

'You are a good soul,' cried Captain Harville . . .

This is the climax. It is very far from passive. Anne's moral idealism is an active quality. It is the rationale justifying her behaviour and refutes criticisms of ineffectual receptivity. It naturally earns her the warm admiration of Harville, and, unknown to her but suspected by us, Wentworth. The debate is central to the novel, and the action endorses its conclusions. If anyone wishes to disagree, they are given the latitude. But Jane Austen is pleasantly convinced of the force and realism of her ending: 'This may be bad morality to conclude with, but I believe it to be the truth . . .'

Conclusion

Elegance

Shakespeare is being translated into 'modern' English. It is very hard to imagine why, except for money. Even so, the language of the seventeenth century does offer problems to the modern reader, and could mislead the idle. Is this true of the language of the early nineteenth century? When in Chapter 4 of *Persuasion* we are told that no second attachment for Anne 'had been possible to the nice tone of her mind, the fastidiousness of her taste', it is conceivable that someone would fail to see that 'nice' is used in its sense of 'discriminating' and that 'fastidious' has no negative overtones, but surely very unlikely. The context, if nothing else, explains the meaning. And the same is even more obviously true when we learn, a few sentences later, that Mr Musgrove's importance is second only to Sir Walter Elliot's 'in that country'. Country must mean neighbourhood or conceivably county, but certainly not England. There are many such instances in Jane Austen, and I suppose they are passed over with unconscious ease.

Nevertheless that ease may itself be the cause of some difficulty. The fact that Jane Austen's idiom contains words familiar to us may lead to missing the particular stress or emphasis which they had for her and her contemporaries. This is especially so in the case of those to do with mental attributes as opposed to those to do with physical facts (e.g. 'fastidious' as opposed to 'country'). No doubt every reader could add to the following list of key words: rationality, cultivation, duty, dignity, decorum, nature, pride, conversation, usefulness, candour, sensibility, benevolence, openness. Here I shall concentrate on one as epitomizing Jane Austen's unique quality. It is very familiar: Elegance. How is it used and how important does it become? In modern English it refers almost entirely to looks, movement, or dress, etc., – to physical things – though it is interesting that scientists and mathematicians have reclaimed it for the intellect by using such phrases as 'an elegant hypothesis' for high and weighty praise.

One of the features, as I have argued, which marks out characters for admiration in Jane Austen is the ability to use language well. In the speeches of Mr Knightley or Anne at their best there is nothing superfluous and nothing wanting. Jane Austen herself is naturally elegant in this way. When, for example, we learn in *Emma* that Mr Elton, successful in love, '... had caught both substance and shadow – both fortune and affection' (Chapter 22), the order and equivalence of the words tells us much more than the mere facts, even though the substance is only about £10,000. But perhaps the best way to appreciate the full quality of elegance is to look first at what it emphatically is not. Henry James, talking of his own work, remarked on 'the general truth, for the spectator of life, that the fixed constituents of almost any reproducible action are the fools who minister ... to the intensity of the free spirit engaged with them' (Preface to *The Spoils of Poynton*). And this could certainly be applied, with a multitude of examples, to Jane Austen. I suppose that in *Emma* and *Persuasion* Mrs Elton and Sir Walter must share the laurels (or whatever leaves are appropriate to their garlands) as dramatic contrasts, or fall-guys, to the main protagonists. This is not a simple matter. Mrs Elton is a genuine threat to Emma in the undiscerning eyes of Highbury. Sir Walter is of course pre-eminent in external elegance – indeed the word is often applied to him with the addition of some such epithet as 'hollow' or 'frigid' or 'heartless'. Even more subtly, other people possess the qualities necessary to elegance without quite *being* elegant. Jane Fairfax is limited only by her forced lack of candour and a corresponding spontaneity and sexiness: otherwise Emma is forced to 'honour, by all her principles ... elegance, which, whether of person or of mind, she saw so little in Highbury' (Chapter 20). Frank Churchill is educated and has an excellent manner. Captain Harville is both strong and sensitive. Admiral Croft has all the benevolence and openness which could be required (children, like dogs a traditional touchstone, adore him). And so on. It is a question of delicate balances. In Chapter 36 of *Emma*, for example, there is a kind of contest between Mrs Elton and Mr Weston as to which can be the most self-obsessed: but a fine differentiation is achieved in favour of the latter because he is concerned with his son and she only with herself. And there is the most acute kind of comedy in the sequence concerning the Coles' dinner party. Emma's first repulsive high-and-mightiness about the possibility of being invited to so presumptuous an affair is quickly turned to a much more loveable anxiety when an invitation fails to arrive. But the easy satisfaction afforded by this spectacle of humbled arrogance is complicated by the worthy Mrs Cole's applause of Jane Fairfax's mysterious piano:

'It has always quite hurt me that Jane Fairfax, who plays so delightfully, should not have an instrument ... This is like giving ourselves a slap, to be sure! and it was but yesterday I was telling Mr Cole, I really was ashamed to look at our new grand pianoforté in the drawing-room, while I do not know one note from another, and our little girls, who are but just beginning, perhaps may never make anything of it; and there is poor Jane Fairfax ...', etc.   (Chapter 26)

This is vulgar and obtrusive and money-proud, however much it may be mitigated by good nature. So Emma, while being unjust, has also been correct.

A concern for *and* penetration of the feelings of others is indeed, as these examples suggest, a vital constituent of elegance. But this does not at all involve the shrinking from rational self-assertion of which Anne Elliot is often unjustly accused. Perhaps it is best defined in action, rather than described. Here is a last example of elegant behaviour and its exact reverse in Mr Knightley's discussion with Mrs Elton of the proposed strawberry-picking at Donwell:

> 'I cannot name a day,' said he, 'till I have spoken to some others whom I would wish to meet you.'
>
> 'Oh! leave all that to me. Only give me carte-blanche. – I am Lady Patroness, you know ...'
>
> 'I hope you will bring Elton,' said he: – 'but I will not trouble you to give any other invitations.'
>
> 'Oh! now you are looking very sly ... Leave it all to me. I will invite your guests.'
>
> 'No,' – he calmly replied, – 'there is but one married woman in the world whom I can ever allow to invite what guests she pleases to Donwell, and that one is –'
>
> '– Mrs Weston, I suppose,' interrupted Mrs Elton, rather mortified.
>
> 'No – Mrs Knightley; – and till she is in being, I will manage such matters myself.'
>
> 'Ah! You are an odd creature!' she cried, satisfied to have no one preferred to herself. – 'You are a humourist, and may say what you like. Quite a humourist. Well, I shall bring Jane ... We are to walk about your gardens, and gather the strawberries ourselves, and sit under trees; – and whatever else you may like to provide, it is to be all out of doors – a table spread in the shade, you know. Every thing as natural and simple as possible. Is not that your idea?'
>
> 'Not quite. My idea of the simple and natural will be to have the table spread in the dining-room. The nature and simplicity of gentlemen and ladies ... I think is best observed by meals within doors ...'   (Chapter 42)

Jane Austen's elegant people resist parodies of themselves by a firm and polite refusal to sink to the level of the mediocre and commonplace society which surrounds them. We can compare Mr Knightley's tranquil obduracy with the vulgar snubs given by the Eltons to Harriet, or the Elliots to Captain Wentworth. The ideal is a quality of mind and spirit hard to achieve but found everywhere in the novels. It is pleasant that in his 'Biographical Notice' Henry Austen describes his sister as a person 'formed for elegant and rational society': it is remarkable that all he says in his eloquent and devoted portrait of a genius should strike the modern reader, so distant in time, as obviously true.

Selected Reading

Primary

1. *The Oxford Illustrated Jane Austen*, ed. R. W. Chapman (6 vols., Oxford, 1923–54). *The* scholarly edition, including the Minor Works (Vol. VI) and lots of useful and intriguing illustrations and appendices.
2. *Jane Austen's Letters*, ed. R. W. Chapman (2nd edn, Oxford, 1952).
3. *Jane Austen: Selected Letters,* ed. R. W. Chapman (Oxford, 1955).

Secondary:

(a) *Life*:

1. *Jane Austen: Facts and Problems*, R. W. Chapman (Oxford, 1948).
2. *The Double Life of Jane Austen*, Jane Aiken Hodge (London, 1972). A sympathetic and readable biography, rather speculative but preferable to more recent and flowery attempts.

(b) *Criticism*:

1. *Jane Austen and the War of Ideas*, Marilyn Butler (Oxford, 1975).
2. *A Reading of Jane Austen*, Barbara Hardy (London, 1975).
3. *Collected Essays*, Vol. 1, Q. D. Leavis, ed. G. Singh (Cambridge, 1983). Contains some uniquely acute writing on Jane Austen.
4. *Jane Austen: 'Emma'*, ed. David Lodge (London, 1968). A 'casebook' which reprints much of the best criticism of this novel up to that date.
5. *Jane Austen: The Critical Heritage*, ed. B. C. Southam (London, 1968). Describes and reprints interesting comments and criticism up to 1870. A second volume (1987) continues the story up to 1940.
6. *Jane Austen: A Collection of Critical Essays*, ed. Ian Watt (Englewood Cliffs, N. J., 1963). Reprints some well-known reactions, including one by Kingsley Amis which neatly illustrates how difficult it is to attack Jane Austen.